The Art of
BIRD CARVING

THIS BOOK IS DEDICATED TO
MY GRANDCHILDREN
ANNE, AMY, and THOMAS

The Art of

bird carving

A Guide to a Fascinating Hobby
by Wendell Gilley

PHOTOGRAPHS BY W. H. BALLARD
and
WOODCRAFT SUPPLY CORPORATION
DRAWINGS BY THE AUTHOR

Published by Hillcrest Publications, Inc.
190 South 100 East
Spanish Fork, Utah 84660
Second Printing, May 1976
Printed in U.S.A.

WENDELL GILLEY
Southwest Harbor, Maine

BLACK AND WHITE PLATES

COLOR PLATES

Contents

Introduction

I must have been born with a jacknife close by as I have whittled since I was a small boy. There is something fascinating about watching a block of wood take on shape as you cut away the chips.

Wood carving is a pastime that is good for the nerves. It is very relaxing and I often get so absorbed that I forget when it is time for dinner. You might almost say it is more fun to whittle than to eat.

I happen to like to carve birds. There are so many different kinds, and each bird is distinctive. The bird carving field is so large that one lifetime wouldn't be long enough to make all of them just the way one would like.

Should you whittle birds for a hobby or as a business, it is still, to my mind, the most interesting work one can do. You can be sure you will never get rich if you carve as a business, but you will have peace of mind that cannot be equalled.

When you make a bird that can be recognized, it is surprising how quickly you can sell it. As you keep making them, you will continue to improve and eventually surprise yourself. If you carve as a hobby, you couldn't find a better avocation, particularly if you like to work with your hands.

Should you decide to try your skill at making a few birds, be sure to bear in mind one thing: "Don't Hurry." Do the work carefully and slowly. It will pay dividends in the end.

I believe that every human being has what I like to call "creative power." The secret is to learn how to release it. Wood carving is an excellent way to set that power in ourselves free.

Wood is a wonderful medium to work with and the possibilities are as great as your imagination. Pick up a slab of pine or some other soft wood, or

1

as many do, try carving a piece of mahogany, walnut or some other variety of hard wood. The main thing is to start somewhere. With patient hands and a few simple tools your bird will take shape. Be it a perfect work of art, or one with a few flaws, it doesn't really matter—it is your creation. What seems important to me is that you have come up with some results, and you have enjoyed doing it. We can't all be masters of the art, but we can be proud that we have created something.

After the bird is carved it has to be mounted on a base of some sort, then painted as near to life as possible. This will also test your skill, and no matter how well you do it, you will always see chances for improvement.

There is no end to the possibilities in making handcarved birds. You can make little birds, large birds, flying birds, and even family groups. You will find that you can devote years to this fascinating hobby without exhausting its possibilities. To date I have carved over six thousand birds, and I still enjoy creating new ones.

In revising my book, I have utilized nearly all of the original volume first printed in 1961. Some things have been changed, and new material has been added. It is my hope that this revision will make enjoyable reading and will help you to carve a better bird.

WENDELL GILLEY
Southwest Harbor, Maine
1972

Foreword

"*B*ull whistler at 2:00 o'clock. Your bird." Wendell Gilley was talking. His gentle down east voice even quieter than usual. I looked high and to the right, into a driving combination of snow and rain, and there, side slipping into the rig of tollers, came the object of Wendell's remarks. If I remember correctly, I missed that particular bird ingloriously on the first two shots and desperately dropped him on the third, but I recall for certain that I thereafter put down my shotgun and did not lift it again until Wendell had done some shooting. This was last fall and for two or three days Wendell Gilley had been telling me that every bird was "my bird" and it didn't make much difference whether he was talking about whistlers over tollers or woodcock in front of a point. I also recall that I had been eating his food, drinking his coffee, wearing his slicker and during the evenings, whittling on his basswood.

That's the sort of trouble you have with Wendell Gilley. I don't know how long ago they coined that phrase "He'd give you the shirt off his back," but they could easily have been thinking about Wendell when they did. I think that one of Wendell's neighbors in Southwest Harbor came closest to the point when he told me that "The only thing Wendell does a better job of than carving birds is being a man." I couldn't agree more with that neighbor and as I muse over this humbling assignment to write a foreword to the new edition of *The Art of Bird Carving*. I realize that my association with Wendell commenced with admiration over 25 years ago when I had yet to reach double figures in birthdays and has continued on just that level ever since.

It started when I literally saved nickels, dimes and quarters to spend on his carvings which, as I recall, were then going for $7.50 in one of this country's most illustrious stores. I don't think that I spent my money on anything else and after eight years of this type of collecting, I wound up owning a set of Wendell's ducks and geese which I still have and which look as good to me now as they did years ago.

It was some time later that I had my next introduction to Wendell, this time through *Bird Carving*. From that moment I began a hobby that to this day gives me the kind of enjoyment that only a fellow wood-carver can fully understand. Like so many others—be they kids, hard working adults or retired old timers—I learned how to carve from *Bird Carving*. My copy is thoroughly dog-eared, stained with raw umber and dark sienna, but is as useful to me today as it was when I made that first tentative cut into a block of wood bearing Wendell's mallard pattern.

Having collected his birds and been instructed from his book, it was not surprising that years later, as a young lawyer, I welcomed an assignment that took me within a few miles of Wendell's home in Southwest Harbor. The timing could not have been better since Wendell had been one of the judges who had recently awarded me one of my first, and hence most satisfying awards, in a decoy contest. I was, in quite a real sense, a grateful student coming to visit a highly regarded master. That visit gave way to many others and led to a friendship with Addie and Wendell Gilley that is of a rare and special nature.

If there is a better book on bird carving than Wendell's I certainly have not seen it, and I can't imagine one coming along that can improve upon it. Although there are many reasons why *Bird Carving* stands alone, these come quickly to mind.

The first is that Wendell has a remarkable directness of style, a simplicity of expression that is absolutely essential (and unfortunately often lacking) in any book that seeks to tell the reader "how to do it." In a nutshell, Wendell's book is easy to read and easy to follow and, therefore, does what it sets out to do and that is, it makes carving easy. I don't think that there is anyone who at one point in his life doesn't yearn to be creative —to sing a song, play the guitar, paint a picture, and yet unless he is lucky enough to be born with some visible talent, is not embarrassed about trying and starting in. Wendell breaks through this barrier and gets the reader carving, and from there on all it takes is practice.

The second reason why *Bird Carving* stands alone has to do with the inventiveness of the author. All one has to do is spend an hour with Wendell Gilley and he will come up with a dozen or more unique ideas that are yet so simple that one finds oneself murmuring "now why didn't I think of that." Wendell's shop is literally jam-packed with tangible evidence of these ideas, many of which are described in this book.

Of course none of this is surprising for Wendell Gilley is no ordinary carver. In fact, he may well be the most highly regarded carver of birds in this country and this takes quite a bit of saying in a decade when this particular hobby has experienced such incredible popularity. But the facts are there. Wendell Gilley has made more than 6,000 birds, birds which are owned by Presidents, Vice-Presidents, Governors, diplomats, corporate executives, judges, doctors, school teachers, boy scouts, beauty queens, lobstermen, dog trainers and Maine guides, to name a few.

This leads me to the third reason why *Bird Carving* is so unique and it has to do with the knowledge and experience of the author. For Wendell Gilley, in addition to being an accomplished bird carver, is a first-rate ornithologist and taxidermist. He knows his birds and applies this knowledge to his carving to the extent that he is not concerned merely in satisfying a potential owner of one of his pieces but in satisfying himself—and this sets one mighty high standard. The toes that Wendell puts on his goldfinches are goldfinch toes, the number of primaries that he has on his ospreys are the number of primaries that ospreys have, the bills on his pintails are pintail bills not blackduck bills. Many times I have watched him agonize over a new species, something which he never shies away from. And this, of course, has lead to an incredible versatility seen not only in the different types of birds that Wendell has carved—I am sure his life list of carvings is longer than the life list of many a bird watcher—but in the shapes, sizes and positions in which he makes his birds.

Wendell Gilley is never in a carving rut. At any given time, you can walk into his studio and he'll be working on song birds, birds of prey, shorebirds and waterfowl. He'll be making a one inch miniature bobwhite quail and a life-size bald eagle. His birds will be swimming, standing, walking and flying. They'll be preening, hatching eggs, sleeping, diving, stretching, and, in short, doing just about everything a bird can do. Yet none of Wendell's carvings are gimmicky or contrived. They have a sense of balance and containment, whether an individual piece or one of his marvelous groups that is so very intangible, so very difficult to achieve and yet so essential to the success of a woodcarving.

If you are reading *Bird Carving* for the first time and are not an old fan who already knows it well, you are in for a very special experience, and I envy you the joy that you will have not just from the book but from the wonderful experience that you will derive from carving—as taught by Wendell Gilley.

DONAL C. O'BRIEN, JR.
Trinity Pass
New Canaan, Connecticut
1972

PLATE 1. Miniature wood ducks completed in 1971.

Wood

*T*here are several kinds of wood suitable for carving a bird. White pine is very good. Cedar can be used, but the grain is coarse and it splits easily. For all-around use I prefer linden, or basswood, as it is commercially called.

Basswood has a very fine grain which holds splitting and breakage of small carved parts to a minimum. It is also free from pitch, which is common to pine. Any wood with pitch grains, if used to make a white breasted bird, will in time show the spots through the paint, and the project is ruined.

Like some woods, basswood varies from hard to soft. Should you purchase basswood at a lumber yard, have them pick out the softest pieces they have. If you cut your own linden tree or basswood and want it to be very light in color, peel off the bark at once.

Two inch thick plank will do for small birds, and, of course, you can get this glued together for larger ones. I usually get my wood at a saw mill, and have some cut 2 inches thick, and some 4 inches thick. The width is determined by the size of the log. As for length, I prefer it in 4 foot pieces. This length is much easier to handle than a real long piece. Once you carve with soft basswood, I am sure you will always use it.

White pine is easy to cut and sands very smooth. It has a sort of built-in oily feeling which makes it pleasant to whittle; but it is apt to have pitch grains which are sometimes hard to detect. A good way to check a piece of wood for pitch is to cut across the grain at about a forty-five degree angle and let it set overnight in a warm place. The heat will cause the pitch to ooze out, and you will be able to see it.

White pine is usually easy to obtain in most areas. Many times you can pick up scraps at lumber yards, furniture factories, carpenter shops, or even when a new house is being built.

I feel that basswood and white pine are probably the two best whittling woods to be used for making birds. In addition, other good carving woods are butternut, cedar, black walnut, mahogany, cherry, and poplar.

After you have the bird carved, you will need some sort of base to mount it on. In fact, I prefer to mount the bird on its permanent base even before it is painted. It can then be removed, painted and replaced. This reduces the handling of a freshly painted bird.

Driftwood, or "dri ki," as it is sometimes called, makes a very appropriate base. This kind of wood is found around the shores of a fresh water lake, or on the ocean beaches. A good place to look for driftwood is an artificial lake or reservoir created by the building of a dam across a stream. Flooding the land behind the dam causes the trees to die and eventually roots and limbs will wash ashore. Some very interesting pieces can be gathered.

PLATE 2. Pile of driftwood.

If you plan to gather driftwood far from civilization, and you often have to go into these places to find good wood, take someone with you. It is a lot more fun that way and is also a good safety measure.

Wood gathered along the ocean is generally called driftwood, while that from a lake shore or pond is called dri ki, and stumps from the forest or seasoned boards from old farm buildings or fences are called weathered wood. I refer to all of it as driftwood.

In selecting suitable pieces for bases, keep in mind how you intend to use them. Avoid diseased and decomposed wood. It is heartbreaking to get a base all made up and then have part of it break off.

I always take a small hand saw on wood hunting trips. There are large chunks that need to be cut up and a saw works best. A hatchet, for example, is apt to break the wood.

Driftwood can be painted, stained or bleached — but all I ever do is brush or wash off the dirt. Warm water and an old toothbrush will do the job.

Before using the wood for mounting bases for birds, trimming is sometimes required. Usually it is best to cut excess wood from the bottom of the piece where it won't show. Since most driftwood contains bits of sand and rock which will dull a power saw in a hurry, use a hand saw for this cutting.

If the piece won't stand by itself, mount it on a board or base. The edges of the base can be rounded off and fluted, roughened by a rasp, or just left plain. Always screw up through the base into the driftwood. Don't try nails as they will not hold well.

The ways in which driftwood may be put to use are tremendously varied and exciting, but the most fun of all is to cruise along the shore of lake or ocean on a sunny fall day looking for a wild tangle of driftwood.

If a driftwood base is not obtainable or wanted, try something else. An attractive base can be made from a flat piece of wood. Saw it in an irregular oval, or a circle, and taper the edges. Sand it fairly smooth, and paint it a dark brown or gray and mount the bird on this.

You might also make a minimum copy of a buoy. These are good for sea gulls and cormorants.

A trip through the woods will many times turn up some very interesting twisted roots or limbs that can be cut and used as bases. Small twigs can also be used to mount smaller birds.

Burls, hard woody outgrowths often found on trunks and limbs of growing trees, make fine bases for mounting birds. They can be easily

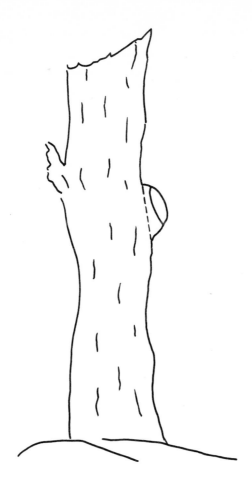

FIGURE 1. Tree with burl. Saw off on dotted line.

removed with a hand saw. I prefer those found on dead trees as the bark has had a chance to dry and the finish is soft and pleasing. When removing a burl from a live tree, no damage will result if you cover the freshly cut surface with thick paint or tar to stop the sap from bleeding.

Leave the bark on or remove according to your desires. To remove the bark, just soak the burl for a few days and then carefully dig off the bark with a dull screwdriver. After the bark has been removed, a wire brush will smooth up the burl and a soft natural finish will result.

Patterns

*I*t is wise to make a pattern of the bird you plan to carve . If the first bird you make from the pattern doesn't suit you, then alter the pattern where you think it needs improvement.

Cardboard is excellent pattern material. Those pieces of cardboard that are in men's shirts when they return from the laundry are fine. The sort of oiled or waxed heavy card in letter files is also good. It holds its edge well. It can be marked around many times before it frays.

Ordinary brown wrapping paper can be used for patterns, but it doesn't hold its shape well.

When making wing patterns for flying birds or spread-winged birds, I prefer thin sheet lead — the kind that is used as flashing material around brick chimneys in house construction. It is about the thickness of cardboard, and can be cut with either a knife or heavy scissors. Make it the shape and size of the wing, and then bend it to the desired position. In this bent position you can hold the pattern above the block from which you are going to cut the wing and mark the side view. Saw this out, and place the lead against the end, and mark and saw out the end profile.

If you are one of the fortunate persons who can draw, or have a friend who can, you won't have a bit of trouble getting a pattern of the bird you wish to carve.

Most of us will have to rely on traced pictures of birds taken from books and magazines. Good bird books are one of the best sources. The covers of sporting magazines sometimes have full color pictures of game birds. Some of these might be interesting to copy. Collect these pictures as you find them. Even though you don't use them right away, you may find them very helpful at a later date.

Mounted birds, if done by a taxidermist who really knows bird anatomy, make good models.

By observing wild ducks and other birds at a zoo, or tame ones in a barnyard, your eye will become trained, and you will be able to judge the accuracy of mounted birds and bird pictures.

The National Wildlife Federation, 1412 Sixteenth St., N.W., Washington, D.C. has some very fine bird prints for sale, and they also have Wildlife stamps that are useful. The pictures are small, but done by very well known artists, and the colors are extremely good. These pictures and stamps are also good to use in painting the bird for color and feather design.

Write them a letter, telling what you desire, and they will send you a list of available pictures.

For pictures of waterfowl, the book *Ducks, Geese, and Swans of North America,* by Kortright, published by Wildlife Management Institute, Washington, D.C., is one of the best.

Find a picture of the bird you wish to make. A side view is best. Lay a piece of tracing paper over the picture and trace the outline. Add a

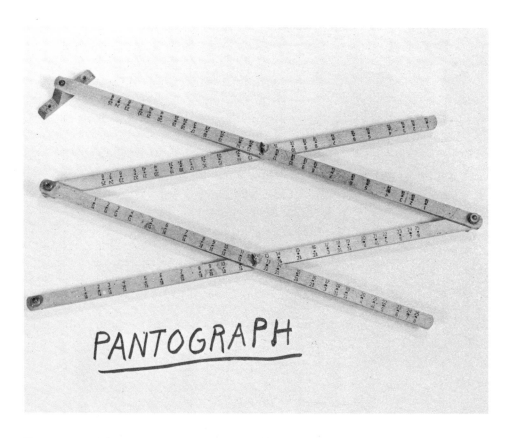

PLATE 3. Pantograph.

little where the wing tips are drawn and possibly at the tail and bill. This will give some excess wood to work on at these points. Remember, you are going to do this in three dimensions, not just a flat profile.

If the pattern you have traced is too large, or too small, you can correct this by the use of a Pantograph. They can be purchased at most art supply stores. The directions come with the Pantograph, and are easy to follow.

You can always enlarge, or reduce, by the squares method.

Now that you have the size profile you intend to use, lay the tracing paper on a piece of cardboard or heavy oiled paper, with a sheet of carbon paper between them, and trace the profile. This will transpose the drawing to the cardboard or paper. With a pair of scissors or a sharp knife and a board to lay the cardboard on, cut out the pattern. Now you have a permanent pattern that can be used over and over, providing, of course, that it suits you.

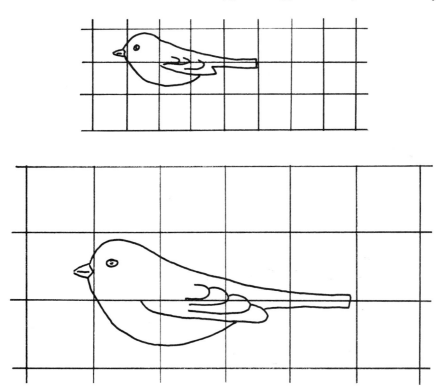

FIGURE 2. Example of enlarging a bird by the squares method.

FIGURE 3. Mallard patterns showing various positions. Enlarge to desired size. Saw out body and head separately and join as shown on hen at top and drake at bottom.

Check the block of wood from which you plan to carve the bird for thickness. Any excess can be trimmed off. If it is too thin, glue two pieces together, and use the glue line as the center line of the bird, vertically.

In gluing two pieces together, be sure that both surfaces are flat, and that they fit together evenly all around. Spread some white glue evenly on both surfaces and clamp them together. Use a vise or carpenter's C clamp. Old fashioned wood furniture clamps are excellent, if you have some.

If you have trouble getting the two pieces of wood flat, so they will fit together and not show a crack in the seam, smooth each side with a carpenter's hand plane to the best of your ability. Tack a sheet of medium grit sandpaper on a perfectly flat surface, such as a bench top. One small tack in each corner should suffice.

Lay the planed side of the block on the sandpaper, and rub back and forth until the block is perfectly smooth and even. Do this to both blocks, then glue them together, and you should not be able to see the seam.

After the glue has set up, place the pattern on the wood block and trace around it. A ball-point pen is really better than a pencil for this. When you position the pattern on the block, be sure the bill or tail is lengthwise

GRAIN OF WOOD THIS WAY

FIGURE 4. Laying out pattern on wood block.

with the grain of the wood. This will make the bird much easier to carve.

After you have traced around the pattern the block is ready for sawing.

If you wish to make a bird with its head turned to one side, it is better to draw and saw out the head separate from the body.In this way you keep the grain of the wood running with the bill. This prevents it from breaking. It is also easier to carve the bill with the grain than diagonally across it .

FIGURE 5. Miniature wood duck patterns. Enlarge by the "squares" method or with pantograph to life-size if desirable.

To attach the head to the body, if you have sawed them separately, cut off a piece of wire, (the wire from a wire coat hanger is good for this purpose) and file or grind both ends sharp. Drill a hole in the neck the size of the wire you plan to use as a dowel, and another hole in the body where the neck fastens on. Insert one end of the dowel in the body, and the other end in the neck, and press together. Be sure of a snug fit. If it does not fit together perfectly, you may have to smooth off the neck, bend the wire dowel, or change the angle of the cut at the base of the neck.

After the two pieces are fitted, just pull them apart slightly, and place some white glue on both wood surfaces: Then push them back together tightly. No need to use a clamp. The dowel will hold it. Wipe off any excess glue and put the piece aside to dry.

A good glue for this purpose is Elmer's glue, or any white glue made from milk products. It sets in a short time, and is very strong. Franklin Titebond resin glue is excellent also.

PLATE 4. Un-sanded body and head of duck, showing placement of pin at neck.

Here are several patterns of birds which I have carved. Study the actual bird if possible before you draw your pattern, or refer to one of the many good books on birds to help you visualize your subject and select a pose which is pleasing to you.

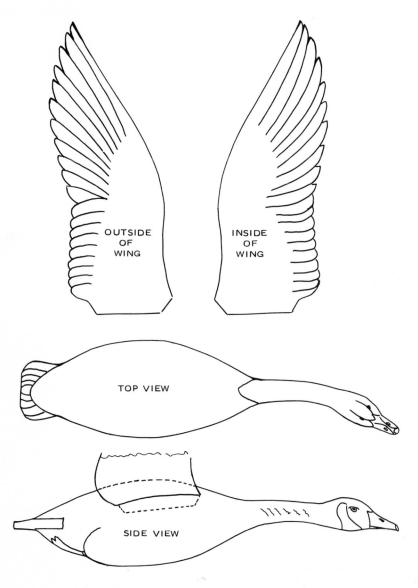

FIGURE 6. Flying Canada goose pattern.

Although most of the song and garden birds are carved to actual size, many of the birds of prey, waterfowl, and upland game birds are carved smaller than life-size. These may be carved to any scale. Perhaps these patterns will be helpful to you in carving a similar bird. They are not drawn

FIGURE 7. Patterns of cardinals.

FIGURE 8. A variety of woodcock patterns. Enlarge as desired.

to any particular scale and can be enlarged as you see fit by either a pantograph or the squares method shown in this chapter.

In the event you wish to design your own carving, and this can give you much satisfaction, these drawings will give you an idea as to how to go about it.

FIGURE 9. Pattern for carving a great blue heron.

FIGURE 10. Owl patterns. Great horned owl (left), miniature screech owl (top) and saw whet owl (bottom). No scale.

Tail

Insert

FIGURE 11. Grouse patterns showing inserted tail section. (Top) Shows tail section made in separate piece. (Bottom) Bobwhite quail patterns.

FIGURE 12. Stylized birds. No scale. Sand and finish natural.

Tools

There are a few power tools that will make the work easier, but they are not a must. Many fine decoys and birds have been carved by the old timers with very simple hand tools. Of course, a great deal of time and effort may be saved with modern power tools. A band saw is one of the most useful, as it can be used for so many different kinds of cutting. It is almost a necessity if you plan to make a great number of life-size birds.

If you have never used a band saw, it would be well to have someone with experience show you how. You must be careful with any power tool, but it is of prime importance that you remember to keep your fingers away from the blade of a band saw.

A jig saw is safer to use, but it is limited as to the thickness of wood it will handle. I have not yet tried one of the new sabre saws, but they could well be satisfactory. Though it is slow, tedious work, you can always fall back on the old type hand coping saw.

Band Saw

For those who would like to have an inexpensive saw that will take 6 inches or more under the throat, I make this suggestion. The Gilliam Tool Co. of St. Charles, Missouri, makes a kit for the do-it-yourselfer. They furnish the metal parts and you make the wood frame and assemble it.

It takes some time and must be done very accurately, but they will send you a full size blueprint showing all the cuts to make and holes to drill. The 12 inch saw will take 6 inches under the throat. This is the size that I made, but I stretched the pattern 3 inches and bought a 6 inch longer blade plus the upper guide bar that comes with their 18 inch model. With this saw I can cut 9 inch thick stock.

PLATE 5. Belt Sander being used on the inside of a wing.

I powered the saw with a 1/3 horsepower motor which is adequate for sawing pine and basswood. The instructions are clear and you should have no trouble building it.

I covered the open side and built a box-like base, cut an opening in the base for the hose of my vacuum cleaner and in this way I collect almost all of the sawdust.

The machine serves my purpose very well. It is not supposed to be a production machine, yet is plenty rugged for the home craftsman.

Belt Sander

A belt sander is very handy, especially for smoothing flat surfaces, such as wings, while a contour sander will do almost any type of irregular smoothing.

In using the belt sander, by placing the fingers of the left hand back of and against the belt, it is possible to sand concave surfaces such as the underside of wings. Do the underside first, then the outside. In this way you are not as apt to oversand the edges, and change the shape of the wing.

If you run short of cloth sanding belts or if you can't seem to find the right width and length to suit you, try making your own. You can buy rolls of metalite cloth in widths of one inch and 1½ inches and from 100 to 500 grit. These rolls can be had in 5 yard or 50 yard lengths. Measure off the length of the belt you need, add ½ inch for lapping, and cut off at a 45 degree angle. Scrape the grit away from the end of the belt that laps over, and cover this scraped part and ½ inch on the back of the other end with glue. Clamp ends together in a vise with waxed paper over the jaws. This keeps the belt from sticking to the vise jaws. Be careful and line the ends of the belt perfectly straight. A crooked belt will not run even. Let it sit over night and the belt is ready for use.

I have made several sanding belts this way and Elmer's or any white glue holds securely.

If you need a ½ inch or 3/8 inch width belt, just tear it off the roll. You can tear it straighter than you can cut it.

Contour Sander

The contour sander is good on round bodies, necks, and hard-to-get-at places. When using a contour sander be sure to keep a firm grip on the bird. The sander turns up so fast it is apt to flip the block from your hands.

These contour sanders are meant to be mounted directly on the shaft of a motor, and most small motors turn at 1750 R.P.M. As this is a little too fast for this type of work, I bought a headstock and mounted the sander on one side, with a 2½" pulley on the other. I put a 1½" pulley on the

PLATE 6. Using a Merit Sand-O-Flex wheel. Photo courtesy of Merit Products, Inc.

motor shaft, with a V belt between the two. This turns the sander at about the best speed for sanding bird bodies.

I made a hood (top of sheet aluminum, sides of wood) to cover the sander, and installed a 1½" tubing connection to the rear. Then I connected my vacuum cleaner hose to this outlet and got rid of most of the sanding dust. A little dust will come out the front, if you happen to hold the work being sanded above the center of the sander.

If you only make a few birds now and then, you can sand them by hand, and would have no use for the sanders or vacuum cleaner.

A very excellent contour sander called the Merit Sand-O-Flex wheel is made by Merit Abrasive Products, Inc., 5515 West 104th St., Los Angeles, California 90009. This sander can be purchased from them, or from most companies that sell carving woods and tools. Woodcraft Supply Co., 313 Montvale Ave., Woburn, Massachusetts 01801, handles these machines as well as many other items of interest to the carver. These sanders come in several sizes. I prefer the No. 350R. Refills of various grits can be purchased. I prefer 100 grit on aluminum oxide cloth, rather than the garnet cloth which is supposed to be used on wood.

Due to the fact that the contour sander is a very simple, but unique tool, I would like to elaborate on it. As a time and labor saving device, I would consider the contour sander just such a tool. This sander can smooth, and I really mean *smooth*, almost any shape object made of wood. It can be used on other materials, but wood is what we are dealing with, so I will confine my comments to it.

It is a round, hollow, metal disc affair, an inch or more thick (according to the size sander) with protruding brushes, in front of which sandcloth projects. You might describe it as a small, straight-sided iron fry pan with a cover, but no handle, and with slots along its sides. The sandcloth does the smoothing, while the brushes back it up for flexibility. It has an arbor on one side, and can be attached to most any slow-speed electric motor, or drill, that turns to the right.

These sanders are made in several sizes. The smallest size is made for hobbyists, and although it will work well on small birds, I prefer the No. 350R for an all-around setup. This is the size I use most of the time, and I can sand a small chickadee or a life-size black duck. The 350R has eight brushes, and does an extra smooth job in a short time.

The sandcloth is fastened to a cardboard cylinder, and unwinds manually as you wear off the working ends. You can unscrew the face and pull out more cloth, and then cut off the worn part with a pair of scissors. Be sure to cut the tabs so they are even in length. They should protrude about ½ inch beyond the brushes. This sandcloth comes in refills of all size grits, and in smooth or fluted bands. The garnet cloth is for use on wood, and the aluminum oxide cloth for plastics, etc. The flat type is for plain sanding, and the fluted for intricate shapes.

I always use the aluminum oxide cloth in flat type on wood, and find it very satisfactory. I prefer from 100 to 120 grit for bird sanding. Coarser grits will cut faster, but won't sand as smooth as the finer type. At times, when I run out of regular refills, I make up my own, using plumber's sandcloth that comes in rolls, and is used for cleaning copper tubing before sweating the joints. This plumber's sandcloth has quite a stiff back, and is made of aluminum oxide with 120 grit. It is quite a little trick to make up one of these refills by hand. The most practical thing would be to get a few different grits and types from the manufacturer. With a little experimenting, you would soon decide just which type you prefer. These refills are inexpensive and can be inserted in the machine in a few minutes time.

It is not absolutely necessary to have the hood and vacuum cleaner that I have referred to, if you do your sanding out of doors in the open air. But as you probably will work indoors you really do need something over the top of the machine, even if it is no more than a flat board. This will keep the dust from flying in your face, as the flaps come up over the back. If you cut a square hole in the bench or whatever you have it mounted on, directly in front of, and below the sandcloth flaps, most of the dust will be forced down on the ground. A cardboard carton placed beneath this hole will catch a lot of it.

The power tools you accumulate will not only make your work easier and faster but will stir up a lot more dust. I build a catcher for dust for each of my power tools and attach my vacuum cleaner hose to it. This eliminates some of the dust problem. There is still plenty the cleaner doesn't get. When using a dust-making tool, be sure to wear a face mask. I always wear one, even with the vacuum, just to be on the safe side. They are sold at paint and hardware stores. If you wear glasses, one of the plastic face shields will help keep them clear and keep the dust out of your eyes.

When using the sander, hold the bird body, or whatever you are smoothing, firmly in both hands, and press it against the sandcloth flaps lightly. The greater the pressure, the faster it will cut, but also the more apt it will be to flip out of your fingers. The way the wheel rotates does not block your vision of the work being done, and you can see exactly how smooth the wood is getting.

Move the work at different angles. On a bird's tail, sand it lengthwise so as not to wear the edges unevenly. Be very careful when sanding near an edge that you wish to keep intact. A piece of masking tape stuck over these places will keep them from being sanded down too thin. A little piece of the tape around the bird's bill will save it, also. Delicate places like the bill should be sanded by hand afterwards.

This little machine can be used to sand the handles of your home-made knives. All told, you will find a multitude of uses for it. It is one machine I would hate to have to get along without.

Engelberg Bench Belt Grinder

This belt bench grinder, made by Engelberg, Inc., Syracuse, New York,

PLATE 7. Engelberg Bench Belt Grinder.

is one of the most useful tools for a bird carver, especially if you plan to make birds with open wings. It is an expensive tool, but will pay for itself in time saved.

The grinder comes with a flat, rubber, grinding wheel. This wheel is fine for flat sanding, but you need a wheel that can be shaped for contour sanding. A composition contact wheel of any desired diameter and thickness can be purchased from Divine Brothers, 200 Seward Avenue, New York, New York.

The composition wheel will fit the shaft of the machine and can be cut to any shape desired with a coarse file held against the wheel while the machine is running. I prefer a convex shape because the belt stays on well and the edge of the sand belt does not dig into the wood—thus a smoother finish. Just take off the outside edges until the face of the wheel is a half circle. This will enable you to use a belt as narrow as ¼ inch regardless of the width of the wheel. Coarse or fine belts 48 inches long can be used. A coarse belt will really cut away the wood.

In shaping a wing, saw out the profile shape on a band saw and if possible saw the contour. This will save a lot of grinding. When sanding on the inside of a wing, work directly on the belt as it passes over the wheel. This will enable you to concave the wing as much as you wish. For the back of the wing, use the belt above the wheel to sand a convex surface. I usually buy a belt 48 inches long by 4 inches wide and with a pair of metal shears I cut different width belts. Just cut a slot the width you need and follow all the way around the belt, but do not cut across the belt. A wide belt is more apt to be found in stock at a hardware store than a narrow one.

This machine can be tipped to an angle or to a horizontal position, and a platen plate comes with the machine for sanding flat surfaces.

If you like the idea of the belt grinder and feel you would like to build one yourself, try your hand at it. This grinder can be used on small carvings of all kinds.

Electric Drill and Bench Grinder

A small ¼ inch electric drill is very handy for drilling holes for leg wires, and for assembly of bases. It can also be used as a disc sander, grinding, and buffing wheel.

I have a makeshift rotary tool, with a hand piece that turns about 300 R.P.M., which I use constantly for drilling holes for wire dowels, leg wires, mounting holes in bases, and for reaming out holes for glass eyes. This tool is about the handiest small power tool in my shop. It was given to me by a friend, and was used originally by his father, who was a barber. It was made for massaging the skin of the face. It had a flexible shaft, so I added a hand piece and was in business.

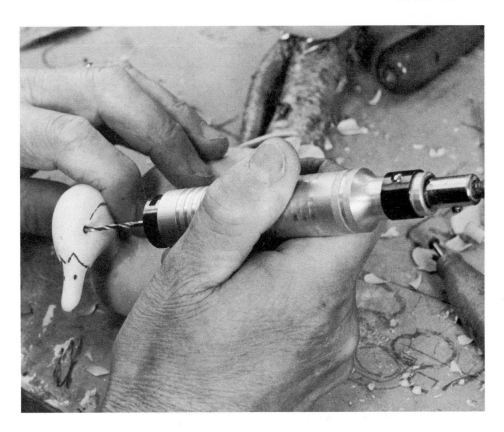

PLATE 8. Small rotary tool and shaft, shown drilling an eye socket.

Most rotary hand tools turn so fast that it is hard to keep from making a slip. One bad slip, and the work is ruined.

It is possible to build a tool of this type by using a regular small motor with small pulley, and a headstock with large pulley, a V belt between the pulleys, and a standard flexible shaft taken off the other side of the headstock. The size of the pulleys would determine the speed of the headstock, and could be changed to suit any purpose.

A grinder and cloth buffing wheel makes sharpening tools a quick job, and it really puts a keen edge on them. If you have a small electric grinder, or a headstock and motor, put a fine grinding wheel on one side, and a cloth buffing wheel on the other.

Grind the blade, or tool, on the stone until you can feel a raw edge on one side. Always keep the blade cool by dipping it often in a can of water kept next to the grinding wheel.

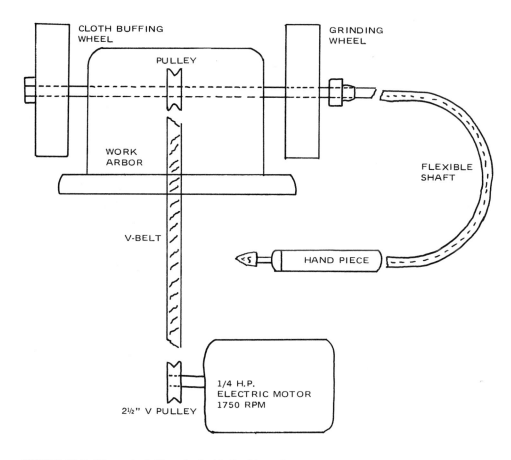

FIGURE 13. Buffing and grinding wheel with flexible shaft rotary tool.

Hold a cake of stainless steel polishing compound against the buffing wheel while it is turning. After coating the cloth wheel with the compound, hold the knife blade—cutting edge down—against the buffing wheel for a few seconds, then reverse position. Do this several times until the raw edge is gone, and you will find you have a very sharp knife, or tool. Stainless steel polishing compound is available at most hardware stores.

As you carve, and the tools get dull, hold them against the buffing wheel now and then. It is not necessary to grind them each time.

Lea Belt Grinder

For sharpening knives, carving tools, chisels, plane-irons, even hatchets and axes, there is nothing better and quicker than a Lea Belt Grinder.

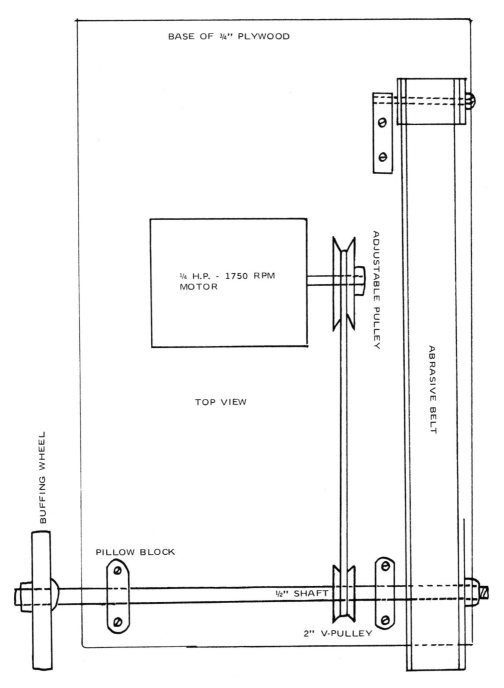

BASE OF ¾" PLYWOOD

¼ H.P. - 1750 RPM
MOTOR

ADJUSTABLE PULLEY

ABRASIVE BELT

TOP VIEW

BUFFING WHEEL

PILLOW BLOCK

½" SHAFT

2" V-PULLEY

FIGURE 14. Drawing of Lea Grinder.

The component parts can be purchased and mounted on a board. If you mount the rubber wheel direct on the motor shaft, you should use a double end shaft motor and use the left-hand side for mounting a cloth buffing wheel. Use stainless steel polishing compound or jeweler's rouge on the cloth buffing wheel. I prefer to have the belt and buffing wheel running away from me, from front to rear.

Another way to assemble this grinder is to buy a piece of ½ inch shafting 18 inches long, two pillow blocks, a 2 inch V pulley for the shaft, and an adjustable V pulley for the motor. This adjustable pulley is the same as that used on a small, forced air heating system fan motor. The pulley can be expanded or retracted and in this way you can control the speed of the belt. Use a fine grit belt for knives and carving tools and a coarse grit belt for hatchets and axes. The component parts for the Lea grinder can be purchased from Frank E. Mittermeier, Inc., 3577 East Tremont Avenue, Bronx, New York, 10465.

Foredom Flexible Shaft Machine

Actually, it is only necessary to have a few tools to make a bird, but after you get started there are so many interesting tools on the market that it is hard to keep from getting a new one now and then.

Recently I purchased from Albert Constantine and Son, Inc., 2050 East Chester Road, Bronx, New York 10461 a Foredom Flexible Shaft Rotary Drill, Series C C hang up type, one tenth horsepower, speed 0 to 14,000 revolutions per minute, with foot rheostat and number 30 hand piece. This hand piece has a key type Jacobs adjustable chuck and will take all size drills and cutters with shanks 5/32 inch or smaller. There are many varieties of cutters and grinders that can be purchased for use in this machine. With them you can drill, saw, or grind wood and soft metals.

Sears Roebuck and Company sells a six piece set of inexpensive rotary cutters with ¼ inch shanks. These cutters are designed in a fluted shape so they cut well but do not dig into the work. The only drawback is that the shaft being ¼ inch will not fit 5/32 inch chuck of the Foredom machine. However, any machine shop will cut this shank down to a smaller size so it can be used. After you have used solder to build up a duck's leg, this cutter will grind it to shape easily and quickly.

Two other advantages of this machine are the small handpiece which can be held easily and accurately and the foot rheostat. The machine is

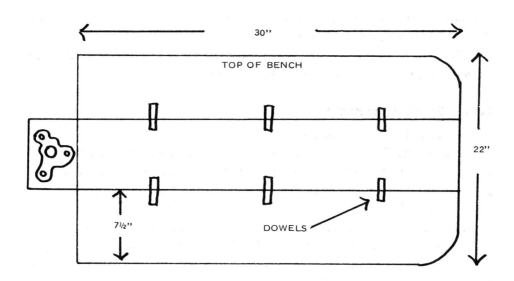

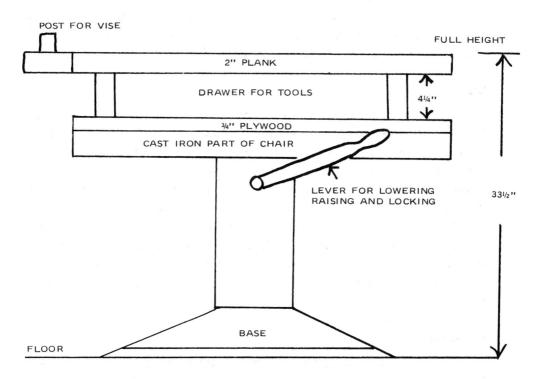

FIGURE 15. Barber chair carving bench.

excellent for making holes for glass eyes, drilling holes for leg wires, sawing slots for open wings, shaping and sanding hard to get at places.

Woodcraft Supply Co. has all types of burrs and files along with a high speed burr grinder that will really remove wood in a hurry.

Barber Chair Carving Bench

If you do a lot of heavy carving and need a sturdy bench that will stand in the middle of the floor, turn 360 degrees, move up and down from sitting to standing height, and also lock in any position, then dig around and find an old discarded barber chair. Remove seat, foot rest, and back rest. The seat will have a flat cast iron base bolted to the top of the hydraulic lift. Build a wood plank bench that can be attached to the cast iron base.

With this bench you can turn the work to you instead of having to walk around it. The weight of the base will hold the bench steady. No need to bolt it to the floor.

This bench is especially useful for carving large eagle plaques, large wings—in fact for carving anything needed to be clamped to a base and held solid. You can mount a vise on one end of the bench to hold smaller carvings.

Vises

There are many fine vises on the market, but I am apt to favor the English made vise sold by Woodcraft Supply. Should you acquire one of these vises, remove the wood jaws and make a new set from oak a little narrower and higher than the original. Cover the wood jaws with some heavy felt. This will hold the bird without slipping or marring the surface. With 3/8 inch felt on the jaws, the vise opens to 6 inches.

If you want a vise that opens exceptionally wide, get an old fashioned bench vise screw with T handle and make one. You can make it to your own specifications. A vise of this type built on the barber chair bench would be excellent for holding life-size bird bodies. I would suggest a felt liner for the jaws.

Chain Saw

I find one of the new lightweight gasoline operated chain saws very handy for many purposes. I always take it with me when gathering drift-wood. With this saw that only weighs 6½ pounds, I can get pieces that I would pass up if I had to cut them by hand. A big chunk of pine or basswood

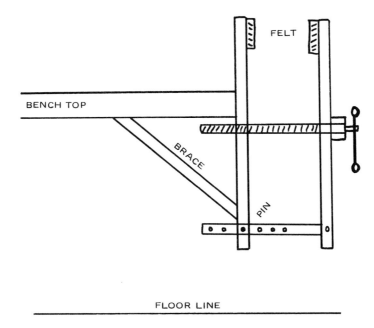

FELT

BENCH TOP

BRACE

PIN

FLOOR LINE

FIGURE 16. Wide jaw vise with felt jaws for holding a carving.

can be cut to size with it, saving a lot of hard work. I have used it to take off excess wood on large carvings.

Knives

If you enjoy whittling, knives will be the tools you are most apt to accumulate. The adjustable handle knife is one of the handiest you can own. The blade can be adjusted long or short, to suit your purpose, and remember that with a short blade there is less danger of getting cut. These are called matte knives, and can be purchased in different sizes, from most art stores. I purchased the ones I have from R. Murphy Company, Ayer, Massachusetts 01432. They manufacture all kinds of knives.

If anyone has trouble or lacks the facility for sharpening tools, I would suggest that they purchase some Xacto knives and gouges. You can discard the blades when dull if you don't want to resharpen them. I use them a lot and always resharpen. In fact, I like them better after regrinding. They are very good, especially for small miniatures and detail carving on wings and bills.

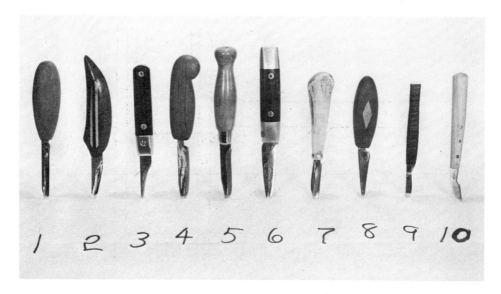

PLATE 9. Collection of knives. 1. Knife made from old straight razor; 2. Knife made from a small thick hack saw blade (Made for me by a friend); 3. A Murphy knife; 4. Knife made from an old straight razor; 5. English knife made in Sheffield; 6. Murphy handle with power hack saw blade; 7. Small knife made from old razor with deer horn handle; 8. Slim taper blade made from old razor (a very handy knife for all cutting); 9. Surgeon's scalpel; 10. Chip carving knife (factory made, good for fine lines and grooves).

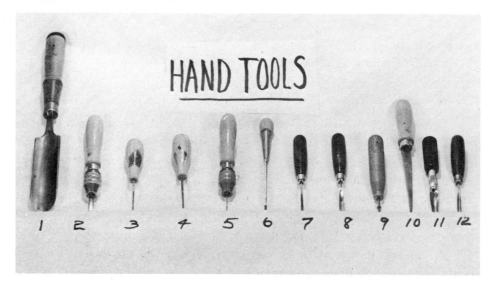

PLATE 10. Hand tools. 1. Large gouge; 2. Small gouge blade held in pin vise; 3 and 4. Small V-tools, one curved, one straight; 5. Large pin vise with drill; 6. 3/16" chisel; 7. Medium size V-tool; 8. Medium size gouge; 9. Tapered reamer; 10. Small key hole saw; 11. Exacto gouge; 12. Small gouge.

If you prefer, you can make your own knives from old-fashioned razors. Your grandfather probably had one that is tucked away somewhere. Remove the razor handle and grind down the tang, tapered so it will fit into a wood handle. To keep from getting cut while doing this, you can wrap the blade in a cloth, or wrap it up with friction tape.

Make a handle to fit your hand. Make it of wood, plastic, or even deer horn. If it is wood, walnut, mahogany, or birch are suitable. Drill two or three small holes side by side in one end of the wood to receive the tang you have just ground down to shape. Place the blade in a vise very tightly. Drive the handle on the tang, driving it firmly, but be careful not to crack the handle. Now you can grind the blade to any shape you like.

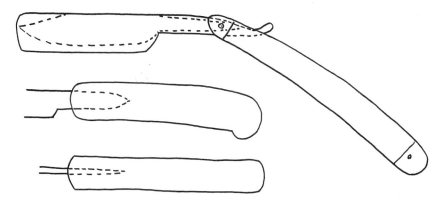

FIGURE 17. Carving knife made from old razor.

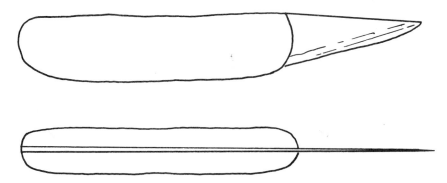

FIGURE 18. Knife made from power hacksaw blade.

Should you wish to make a knife and can't find an old discarded razor, a small power hacksaw blade will serve the purpose well. Grind off the saw teeth and glue the blade between two pieces of wood. Use almost any kind of glue—epoxys are best. Clamp the handle in the jaws of a vise until dry, then shape it to fit your hand. After the handle is finished, grind the blade. Most of these blades are made of self-tempering steel and will not lose their temper if you over heat them in grinding.

Always wear a face guard when grinding tools. A small piece of steel in the eye could result in loss of vision.

When you use an electric emery wheel, or grinder, be sure to have a can of water handy, and keep dipping the blade, as it heats up from the grinding. Grind very slowly, because if the blade gets hot enough to turn blue, you have drawn out the temper and it will be too soft to hold a good keen edge. It could be re-tempered, but this is a job for an expert.

A regular pocketknife is all right to use, but I never cared much for them. Most of them have small handles that cramp the hand. The blades are apt to be pretty soft steel, and the angle of the blade never seems to be just right. You also have to be careful about them closing, which might result in cutting yourself.

To enjoy whittling, or carving, you must have a very sharp knife. To sharpen it by hand on a flat oil stone, just put some oil on the stone and rub the blade back and forth from toe to heel, first on one side, then on the other. Do this until you can feel a raw edge on one side of the blade.

Strop the blade, the same as you have seen a barber strop his razor. Do this on a piece of leather, tacked or glued to a flat board. Rub some jeweler's rouge on the leather, and it will make the blade sharper.

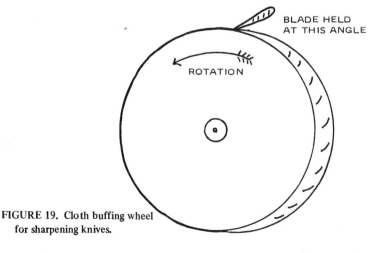

FIGURE 19. Cloth buffing wheel
   for sharpening knives.

Continue to strop until the wire edge has disappeared, and the knife should be in good condition to carve with. As your knife gets dull from carving, just strop it a few times on the leather.

You should have a medium sized gouge, about ¼ inch or 3/8 inches wide, and a fine V tool. A good V tool is the type used in checkering gun stocks. This V tool is handy for cutting feather lines. It is an extra small size

FIGURE 20. Fish tail gouge. No scale.

A fish-tail gouge (as it is called) almost one inch wide, and with just a little curve from the flat, is a fine tool for cutting the underside of wings.

A 2 inch wide regular butt chisel can be used to rough carve the bird body.

Many hardware stores have rifflers, or wood files. These are useful in smoothing hard-to-get-at spots. They are made in various shapes. You should have a regular wood rasp, to use at times for smoothing the carving before sanding.

A real handy tool for smoothing hard-to-get-at places is a regular 10 inch rat-tail file. If you should want it curved, just heat it red hot, and bend it to the desired shape. Heat it again cherry red, and dunk it in water. (Cool it quickly.) This will harden it, as it was, originally. No harm if you don't retemper it, as long as you are just rasping wood, but should you want to trim down some built-up solder or fiberglass cement, it would dull pretty quickly. These files are fairly coarse, and they cut fast. They are excellent for cutting down fiberglass.

A long thin shingling hatchet is great for roughing out a large bird body. Sharpen it as you would a knife, and cut the handle to about 10 inches overall. This makes for better control. Use it as a hatchet or grasp it near the head and use it as a chisel.

While we are on the subject of tools, I made a very simple little sander that has worked out fine. I suggest you make one in your spare time. You will find many uses for it. Make the blade from a piece of plumber's

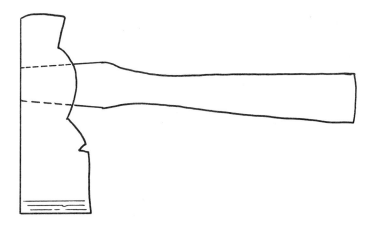

FIGURE 21. Long blade hatchet.

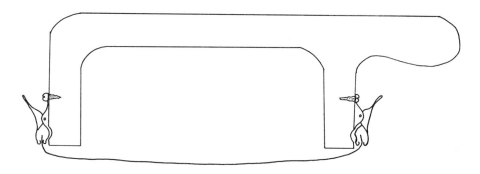

FIGURE 22. Hand sander, 3½" high by 12" long. Strip of sand cloth (any width) is held by two small spring clamps.

sand cloth, or any aluminum oxide cloth. I cut the cloth in ½ inch strips.

Don't try to put the sand cloth on too tightly. It will sand round objects better if a bit loose.

Dust around a shop is a nuisance, and to get rid of it I use a commercial type vacuum cleaner—the kind made for cleaning furnaces and heating systems. It is a tank type with a 1½ inch flexible hose. I attach the hose to all my power tools, and in this way eliminate about 90 per cent of the dust. My shop is small, and I just cannot have dust in the air, especially since I do my painting in this same room.

There is a tool called a Bench Holdfast. The one I have was made in England, and I purchased it from the Woodcraft Supply Co. It will hold

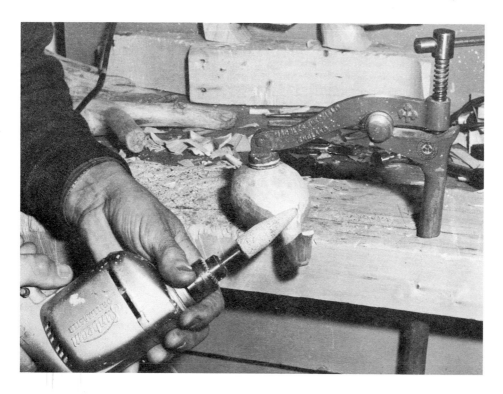

PLATE 11. "Bench Holdfast" tool used to clamp roughed-out bird to bench while the cone-shaped carborundum grinder, used in the electric drill, grinds the finish into the breast of an American eider duck.

almost anything in a fixed position while it is being worked upon. Just bore a hole in the top of a bench, or in the plank that is clamped in the vise and used to rough-cut on, and insert the shaft of this tool. As the screw is tightened, the pressure of the holding arm throws the shaft off perpendicular so that it rigidly binds in the hole. You can easily remove it when not in use. It is especially good for holding bases while making groove cuts with a gouge. The little round hold-down on the lever arm has a fluted base, and makes marks on the work. To overcome this, I glued a small, round piece of masonite hardboard to this surface with some epoxy cement. It hasn't come off yet, and it doesn't mar the work.

To summarize, here is a list of the tools that are really necessary to make a bird: A knife of some sort with a blade of good steel; blade should be about 2 inches long by 3/8 inches wide and tapered to a point; a small hand drill, with several assorted drills to correspond with the wire sizes used; a pair of flat-nose cutting pliers about 5 inches long, and large enough to cut a wire coat hanger; a pair of small scissors for cutting sheet lead; a small anvil, or old flatiron, to hammer on; a small tack hammer; a hand coping saw (if you don't have a power saw); a carpenter's hand saw, most any size; a small jeweler's saw with very fine teeth and reinforced back, similar to the type made by Xacto. This saw is used to trim and cut necks, and needs to be sharp and fine. A few files, both flat, round and half-round are also necessary. The ones used for filing lead should be the bastard type. Include a fine flat file for sharpening wires.

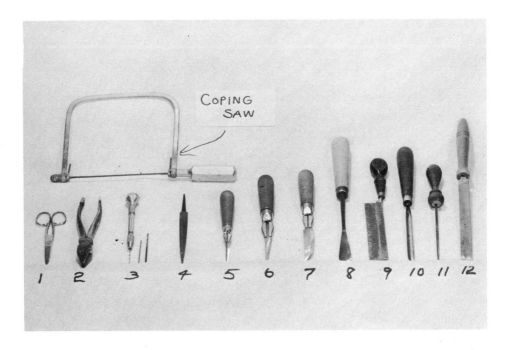

PLATE 12. Necessary tools. 1. Small scissors; 2. Wire cutting pliers; 3. Small pin vise and drills; 4. Flat file; 5. Adjustable handle knife No. 00; 6. Adjustable handle knife No. 0, with regular blade; 7. Adjustable handle knife No. 0 with oversize hand-shaped blade for concave cutting; 8. Fish tail gouge; 9. Jeweler's saw; 10. Medium gouge; 11. Small rat tail file; 12. Regular fine flat file.

With these tools, plus some sandpaper, wire, wood, paint, and a little patience, you are equipped to make a wooden bird including metal feet and wire legs. Other tools which I have mentioned will make the work more interesting and will probably speed it up some, but speed is not required. It is better to progress slowly and carefully. The bird you make will be better because of it.

Sawing Out Models

*N*ow that we have drawn the pattern, let us saw out the model we intend to carve.

If you plan to make many birds, a band saw is a must. You may have a friend who has a band saw you can use, or you can get them sawed out at a shop that does millwork. If someone does this for you, be sure they follow the pattern lines very accurately.

PLATE 13. Sawed out blocks of flying gull, chickadee, flying goose and mallard.

To use the band saw, set the gauge of the saw just above the wood block. I use a ¼" blade for large birds, and 1/8" blade for smaller ones, say the size of a chickadee. Follow the lines with the blade. Don't try to turn the work too short. If the saw binds, back the work off and cut in at another angle. Always keep your hands and fingers out of line of the cutting blade. Pay full attention to what you are doing; don't let anything distract you! If someone approaches to speak to you, turn off the motor. If you must wear a necktie, let it be a bow tie. Any loose clothing is dangerous. It could easily get caught in the machine.

After you have sawed out the profile, mark the approximate top view, and just saw away some of the surplus wood. I sometimes hold the bird firmly, and saw off a little of the excess wood, especially on each side of the neck. If you wish, you can cut this surplus away with a knife, and in this way you should be able to shape the body more accurately.

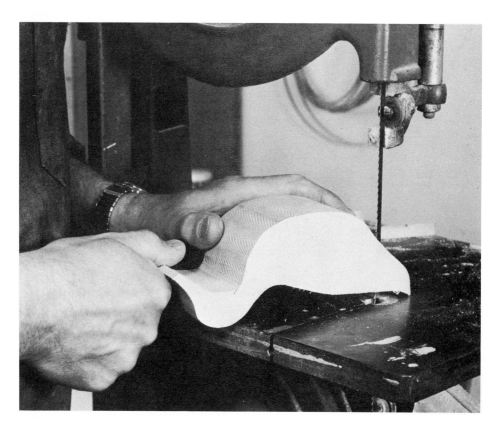

PLATE 14. Excess wood being removed by band saw.

Some bird carvers saw out their patterns in what is referred to as compound cutting. First they saw the profile, then replace the pieces cut off, and saw out the top view. This is good, but each bird has to be marked out and sawed from a single block. Also, the block must be square on all four sides. To save wood, I stagger the patterns on a large plank, and sawing them out is sometimes like sawing a jigsaw puzzle.

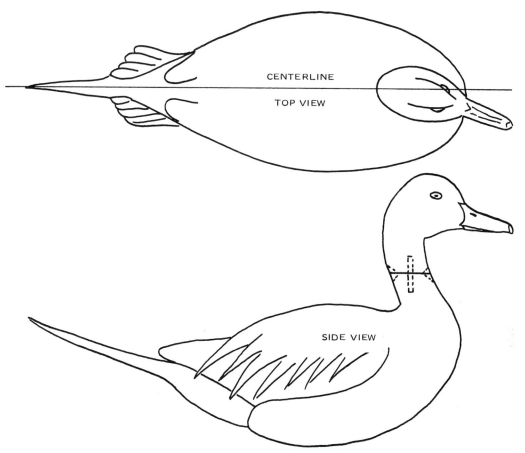

CENTERLINE

TOP VIEW

SIDE VIEW

FIGURE 23. Pintail pattern. Neck and head are joined with dowel and joint is filled with plastic wood.

Before you start carving make a pencil line all around the center of the sawed-out model. This line should be lengthwise of the bird in the verticle plane.

While you are whittling, never at any time cut any of this mark away. This line will keep the same profile you planned when you made the pattern.

After completing the carving with the knife, you can then remove the center line with sandpaper, as you smooth up the model.

Probably the first bird you make will have its head straight to the front, as you had it marked and sawed. Should you wish to have the head turned, cut off the neck with a jeweler's saw. If the bird has a ring around the neck, similar to a mallard drake, cut on this line. The cut won't show as much, if done this way.

Drill a hole in the body at the center where the neck attaches, and one in the center of the neck. Insert a piece of wire in these holes, place some white glue on the wood, and press together tightly, setting the head at

PLATE 15. (top) Mallard carved, ready to sand. Note centerline used during carving. (right) Cardinal with wing feathers and bill carved. Note one leg wire in place. (left) Wood duck with primary feathers lifted from body and set in place. (Note: The shallow cuts for feathers and bill lines are blacked in on the models to assist in showing location and shape.)

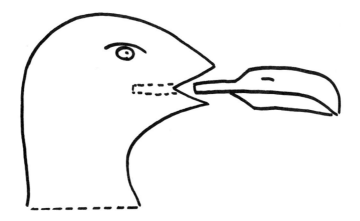

FIGURE 24. Sea gull head drilled to receive new bill. Bill is made in the form of a dowel.

the desired angle at this time. It is wise to have the drill the same size as the wire to insure a tight fit. A piece of wire coat hanger, sharpened on both ends, makes a good dowel. A nail with the head filed off is also good. On very large birds, say a life-size duck, a hardwood dowel is best.

You can change head positions, add wings and tails, and even replace a bill that is across the grain of the wood, or broken off. To add a new bill, just saw one out to shape, then shape it with a knife, leaving a piece of wood shaped like a dowel attached to the base. Saw off the old bill, drill a hole for the dowel, and glue it in place.

Carving

*N*ever try to carve with dull tools. In holding a knife for carving, you should grip it in such a way so that if it happened to slip, the blade would not cut your hand, or your leg, if you had the work in your lap. I find that a very good way is to grasp the knife with the right hand as a lever to force the cuts. This gives good control of the knife blade, and also the sharp edge of the blade is away from you, so that if it should slip, no harm would be done.

This procedure can only be used on birds that are small enough to hold in one hand, and still have freedom of the left thumb. Hold the knife in the most comfortable position for you, but watch out for the sharp edge of the blade. The least little slip—and a badly cut finger!

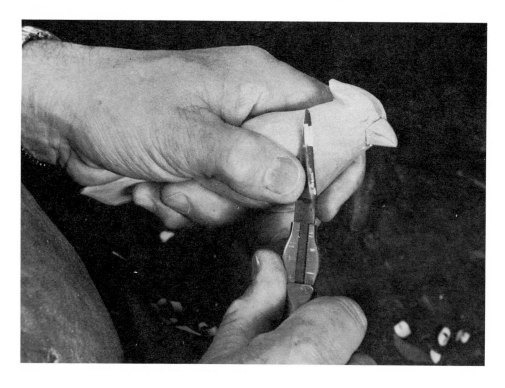

PLATE 16. How to hold knife, using thumb of left hand for pressure.

I know a fellow who was carving the links of a wooden chain, with the wood he was working on resting in his lap. His knife slipped and cut right through his pants into his leg, and he had to have the doctor take three stitches in the cut.

After you have sawed out the pattern of a large bird, say a goose about eight or ten inches long, you will find it advantageous to rough away some of the surplus wood before getting down to the more accurate carving. A good way to do this is on a piece of two by six plank, fastened in a bench vise. This plank will come in handy many times, and is well worth the trouble of making. A chopping block could be used instead of the plank, if it is easier to obtain.

By resting the work to be carved against the plank, and using a good size knife—say a 4" blade, ¾" wide—cut away the surplus wood. As the knife blade cuts off the larger chips, let the blade hit against the plank. This allows you to put more pressure on the knife without danger of cutting

PLATE 17. Rough carving with chisel.

yourself. It could be called using a hatchet in slow motion. A regular hatchet could be used with the plank as a block to chop away the excess wood. While this method is fast, it is not accurate, and more wood might be removed than is planned. I do not recommend the hatchet except for bulky birds about 12 inches long or over, and then only when using a knife would be too hard on the wrist and arm.

A coarse rasp will wear away the excess wood and bring the carving to shape, though it is a slow procedure. But it is a very safe way, and the carving would have to be held in a vise so that both hands could be used on the rasp. When I have a large bird to trim down. I hold it against the plank with my left hand, and with the knife in my right hand chip off chunks of wood small enough so it does not tire my wrist.

After you take off some on one side, turn the bird over and do the same on the other side. Try to keep both sides even. It will help later on when you start to carve more accurately.

PLATE 18. Use of plank in vise for rough carving.

With the carving in your left hand, and the knife in your right, start shaping it to resemble the model you are working from. Take small cuts with the grain of the wood. It will be necessary to keep turning the body as you carve, first one way, then another, so that the knife blade will cut angling *with the grain* and not against it.

Take a little off on one side, turn the bird over and take the same amount off the opposite side, but never cut away the center line you have marked on the carving. Study the model from time to time, and be sure not to take off too much in any one place. It is better to have a little excess wood than to take off too much and spoil the project. Even after the bird is sanded, if you think it is too fat just take a knife and trim that part away. It is wise to study the general anatomy of the bird you are planning to make. If you know the shape of the bird in real life, you are better able to judge when you have it correctly carved and ready for sanding.

I find that if I am making a bird that I am not familiar with, I will

PLATE 19. Sea gull with crossed wing tips. Note the centerline carving guide.

carve it roughly to shape, sand it to get more of an idea how it is going to look finished; then I carve it again, taking off the parts that look as though they shouldn't be there.

I feel it is best to leave detail work such as wing, feathers, and bill until after the bird is all smoothed up. This may seem like extra work, but you will find that you can shape them better, and sand the edges smoother.

There is usually a depression where the eye sets in a bird's head (especially the ducks'). If you carve in this notch before setting the eye, your bird won't have a pop-eyed look. Hawks and eagles have a prominent over-hang above the eye.

A bird's back should be arched, some more than others. A sagging back will spoil the looks of your carving. Another thing to remember: when you install the leg wires in the body, don't set them too far to the rear.

FIGURE 25. Face of hawk

A bird balances its body evenly on its feet. Many taxidermists make the mistake of getting the bird's feet too close to its tail. The loon family does have its legs way back, but they don't walk well, and when sitting usually assume an upright position, letting the feet and legs act as a lever.

If you are making a small bird, such as a chickadee, life-size, or a miniature duck about 4 inches long, you can, if you desire, sand it smooth and paint the wing feathers on. On a bird of this size it is hard to tell at a glance if they are carved, or merely painted. Carving does give a shadow that painting does not. A larger bird needs the wings carved to make them stand out. This can be done with a V tool or a knife. Mark the wing feathers with a pencil. Make a vertical knife cut along the line, then a horizontal cut to take out the wedge-shape piece of wood. Make these cuts very shallow.

If by chance you want the primary wing feathers lifted from the body, carve them out and after sanding the body, insert them into the bird's body, the same as you would a wing. Cut a slot and insert the wing feathers, gluing them in place. Then fill the depressions with Plastic Wood or Duratite Wood Dough, and sand off the excess after the dough has set.

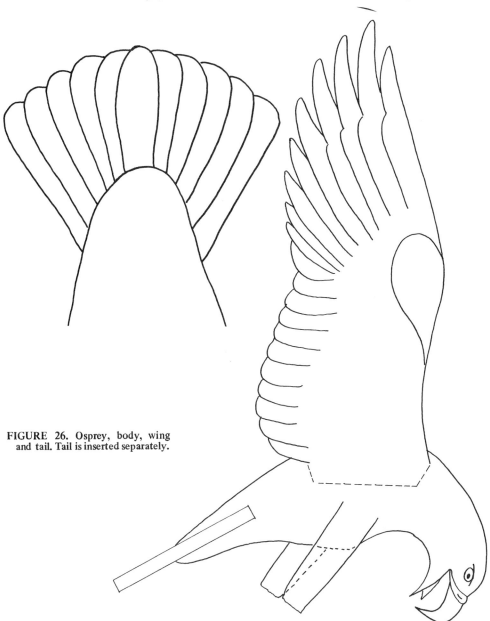

FIGURE 26. Osprey, body, wing and tail. Tail is inserted separately.

PLATE 20. Osprey.

If you wish, make a model of the wing tips out of sheet lead, and carve the wood ones from these. Some bird carvers use sheet metal, such as brass or tin for wings and then paint them. I have done it on small terns whose wing primaries are long and slender, and could easily be broken.

A sea gull has such long primary wing feathers that when the bird folds its wings, the tips usually cross each other. At first, it is hard to carve these crossed wing tips, but with patience and careful cutting, you should have no trouble. Notice, too, that their wings extend beyond the tail.

There are times when you may wish to spread the bird's tail wider than the thickness of the piece of wood you are carving the body from. This is very true in the case of the osprey. Saw out the body, and saw a slot where the tail would normally be. Insert a thin, wide, piece of wood, and carve to shape.

PLATE 21. Small tern with metal wings. (bottom) Leg wires inserted and bent.

Burning

An easy and effective way to put the feather lines on a bird is with a small electric burning pen. The idea of burning was brought to my attention by a friend in Arizona. I had seen some burning several years ago. At the time I thought it was done with a very fine V tool. I didn't realize the feather marks were burned in. I had a burning pen, but hadn't used it much. Now I am beginning to wear it out. My friend from Arizona sent me a burning pen and told me about the idea. After experimenting for a while, I found that it seems to work best if the bird is primed with Gesso and the marks burned into it instead of trying to burn the bare wood and have the marks partly filled with paint when the bird is primed.

The best subjects for burning are eagles, hawks, woodpeckers, and owls and most life-size models. The smaller birds do not lend themselves quite as well to burning, but I have burned the feathers on chickadees with good results.

PLATE 22. Inside wing of Canada goose coming in for a landing. Shows burning marks.

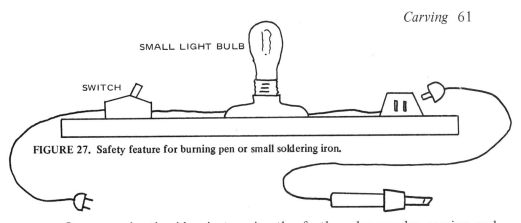

SMALL LIGHT BULB

SWITCH

FIGURE 27. Safety feature for burning pen or small soldering iron.

On an eagle, the idea is to raise the feathers by regular carving and then burn in the shaft and small quill feathers. On a duck where the feathers are smooth, outline each feather with a pencil and bear down heavily, then burn in quills. On the ducks breast, make a lot of straight marks similar to those made by a machinist's tap. A little trial and error will produce the results you are after. Many burning pens have interchangeable tips. For the average burning, I prefer a tip shaped like a skew chisel. Round the burning blade a bit and you won't be as apt to dig into the wood. Gesso burns easily, so a steady firm stroke is best. These burning pens can be obtained from hardware or toy stores. A 24-watt pen is usually sufficient for average burning. As a safety measure, so that I would not leave the iron with the electricity on, I made up a base with switch, light bulb, and plug in adapter. When the pen is turned on, the light comes on and burns all the time I am working with the pen. A 7½-watt bulb is ample. The idea is just to keep you aware that the burning pen is on. A fire could result if you set the pen aside still connected with electricity.

This base with switch and bulb can be used along with a small electric soldering iron as a safety measure.

After I have burned in the feather marks, I find it advisable to give the bird a light sanding with fine sandpaper just to smooth out any marks that have raised the edges in the Gesso. For fine lines, keep the edge of the pen sharp by lightly rubbing on a flat piece of very fine sandpaper.

Gesso is a water base primer and does not gum up the burning pen; cleaning now and then with sandpaper will keep it working well. In time heat will darken and corrode the tip.

Burning is a slow and time-consuming task, but after the bird is painted the results are worthwhile.

You can purchase excellent burning pens from Albert Constantine Co., 2050 Eastchester Road, Bronx, New York 10461.

Sanding

$\mathcal{A}$fter the bird model has been carved to shape, and is fairly smooth, it needs to be sanded with either sandpaper or sandcloth. Normally, you will do this by hand. On a small bird, I take a piece of about No. 80 grit sandpaper or sandcloth, that measures approximately 3 inches long by 1½ inches wide, and fold it lengthwise so that the sanding surface is about 3/4 inches by 3 inches. Using this under the right thumb, go over the entire bird, sanding off all bumps and depressions. The bird will still be rough. Change to a finer grit, say No. 120, and go over the carving again. The bird should become very smooth and even.

If by any chance the roughness of the sandpaper hurts your thumb, get a small piece of rubber rug anchor (which can be purchased at any furniture store) and place this between the thumb and sandpaper or sandcloth. I prefer aluminum oxide sandcloth for the final sanding. It is more flexible than paper, and the edge holds up better when folded. The rug anchor won't slip on your thumb or on the sandcloth.

If you have a tough place to sand, say under the curved wing of a flying goose, and the sanding happens to be on the end grain of the wood, I think this little trick will solve the problem.

Insert a long, cone-shaped carborundum mounted grinding wheel (the kind that has a metal shaft protruding) in the chuck of a 1/4 inch electric drill. Use this to grind down the wood, as you would if it were metal. Move the stone back and forth as you grind, and it is surprising how smooth a finish you will be able to get. It is slow work, but saves a lot of rubbing with sandpaper.

If I were making a large bird with a white breast, and wanted the finish smooth, but a little uneven, I would go over it with one of these stones

62

right after carving it with a knife. I would use no sandpaper on the breast, and when painted, the effect is unbelievable.

It will be necessary to trim the bill to shape, and make the cuts where the base of the bill joins the head. With a small knife carefully cut the bill to its final shape, and sand smooth. Make sharp cuts at the base of the bill, and sand smooth. This is a good time to mark the primary wing feathers, and cut them with a knife or V tool. You can mark and cut each individual primary feather. This is a matter of preference. If you carve them, there will be no need to paint the fine lines to show up the individual feathers. The carved lines will cast a shadow, and look very realistic. Just don't carve these individual feather lines too deep. In fact, keep the cuts as shallow as you can make them. With the rough edge of the sandcloth, smooth all the edges of the cuts you have made.

After the bird is smooth and ready for a coat of primer, such as

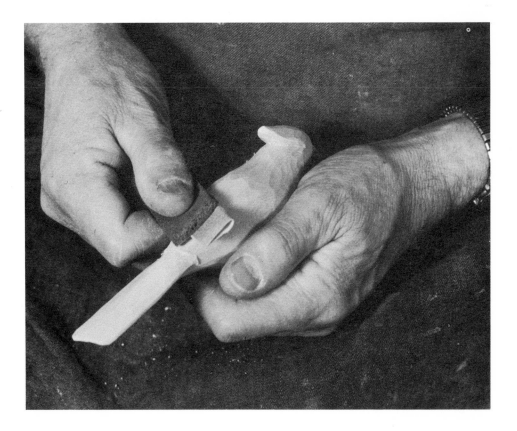

PLATE 23. Hand sanding a cardinal.

Firzite, there is one more operation to perform, if you have glued the head on separately. Make a V cut around the neck, using the glue line as the center line. Do this with a knife, or a small rasp, or V shape riffler or wood file.

Fill in the V groove with Plastic Wood or Wood Dough. Press the plastic wood in firmly, using the thumb and forefinger. After the Plastic Wood has hardened at least 24 hours, trim the excess and level off with knife. Then smooth with fine sandpaper or sandcloth. If you make the joint in this way, the joint can be covered when you paint the bird so that it will not show.

It is very tricky to glue two pieces of wood together (a butt joint) so that the seam does not show when painted. Thus the reason for the V cut, and the filling with Plastic Wood.

I have tried all types of wood fillers, and I like Plastic Wood or Wood

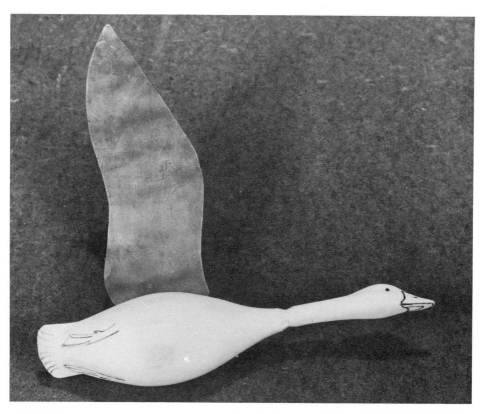

PLATE 24. Flying Canada goose. Note cuts at base of bill, outlining of legs and feet, and V-cut on neck after bird has been sanded. Method of bending lead pattern for a wing illustrated. (Note: The fine and shallow cuts for feathers, etc. are blacked in on the model for better delineation of location and shape.)

Dough best. It will shrink some upon drying, but not enough to bother.

If you are fortunate enough to have a Sand-O-Flex, it is surprising how much of the hand labor of sanding can be done on it. I can sand almost all of a chickadee, with the exception of the bird's bill. When sanding close to the bill, I put the thumb of my left hand over it to keep the tabs of sandcloth from hitting it and wearing it out of shape. Then I shape and sand the bill carefully by hand. It is also good practice to be careful on thin places, such as the tail. Hold the model lightly against the sander when doing these delicate parts. Always sand the heavy, thick parts first.

A very good sandcloth is the roll type used by plumbers for cleaning copper tubing. With a pair of scissors you can trim off pieces any length you desire. The grit is fine enough to do a good smooth job.

Alcohol Treatment

After you have sanded a bird it will be smooth, but sometimes you want it to be smoother still. In that case, spray the sanded bird with denatured alcohol in a plastic spray bottle or window cleaner bottle. This spraying will raise the grain to a soft velvet surface. After it has dried, sand with number 320 wet and dry sandpaper. The results will amaze you. The wood will be nearly as smooth as glass.

Wings

*T*he first step in making a pair of wings for a flying or spread-winged bird, is to draw them out full length on a piece of cardboard or heavy paper. Transfer this drawing to a piece of thin sheet lead, the same shape as the drawing.

You should have the bird's body all shaped and sanded at this time. Cut two slots in the body where the wings attach, about one half inch deep. Insert the lead wing in each slot; first one and then the other. The same lead pattern can be used for both wings. Just bend it the opposite way. No need to make two patterns, unless you wish.

Hold the bird up and bend the lead to the contour you wish for the finished wood wing. Remove it from the slot, being careful not to move it out of shape. Hold the lead pattern above the wood block, and mark out the shape from the side view.

Keep the primary wing feathers with the grain of the wood. Saw out the pattern you have drawn and, if it suits you for shape, place the lead pattern endwise on the block and draw the curve, or end view of the wing. Draw two lines, the outside, and underside, of the wing. Be sure to saw the wing a bit thicker than you will want the finished product. It will need to be curved or convex, on the top, and dished out, or concave, on the underside. When you bend a wing, you shorten it, and the lead pattern shows just how much. The slots you make in the body for the lead wing will have to be made wider later on to accept the wood wing, which will be thicker than the lead model.

Another way to make a curved wing, and probably a simplified way: Mark out the curve on a block of wood of ample size. Keep the grain of the wood with the wing tips. Saw out this line, then using a pair of dividers, set at the thickness you want the wing, scribe another line parallel with the first line. Saw along this line. The result will be a longitudinal section.

Now lay the lead pattern on this piece, mark around the lead and trim to the wing shape. You may have to either saw this line by hand, or cut·

FIGURE 28. Flying herring gull showing side and end view of wing.

it with a knife, as the curve is hard to get up to the band saw blade without cutting off part that is needed. You can use a small hand coping saw for this, or regular carpenter's saw.

With a knife, or rasp, shape the outer side of the wing as near the shape of a bird's wing as possible. Sand it smooth, then place it on the carving

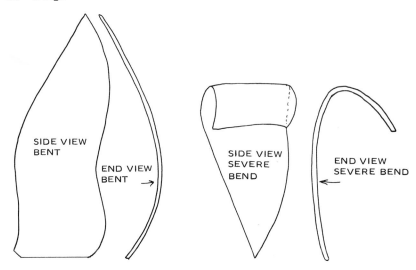

FIGURE 29. Patterns of lead wings bent to different shapes.

PLATE 25. Flying Canada geese.

block against a small wood cleat nailed or screwed to the block. With a gouge in your right hand, and holding the wing with the left hand, and cutting crosswise to the grain, hollow out the underside of the wing. Do this slowly and carefully, being very careful not to let the gouge slip. Take off only a small chip of wood with each cut. You will need to turn the wing end for end, at times, as you work.

Get this as smooth as possible, as it will save a lot of sanding. Trim down any bumps and high spots with a round nosed knife, then sand smooth. For sanding the underside of a wing, use the rug anchor to protect and cushion the thumb. Now mark off the primary and secondary wing-feathers with a pencil.

Most birds have ten primary feathers on each wing, so don't make any more. Looking down on top of a wing, the first primary feather is under the second, and so on. In carving these feathers, be sure to make the cut

PLATE 26. Use of gouge on the underside of wing.

showing them in this position — that is, from the top you don't see the back edge of the feather. The back edge only shows from the underside.

After they are carved to shape, the wings can be sanded by hand, the same as you did the body. If you have a belt sander, this is a good time to use it.

Mark off the primary and secondary wing feathers on the outside of the wing, and with a knife cut straight in on the marks, about the depth of the thickness of a sheet of paper. This straight cut will be the front edge of the feathers. Then cut in lightly at an angle, and remove a small wedge shaped piece of wood.

With the folded edge of a piece of sandcloth or sandpaper, smooth the surfaces of these cuts. Mark the feathers on the underside of the wing, to correspond with the outside cuts, and finish these in the same manner. Widen the slots in the body, and insert the wood wings for a good tight fit.

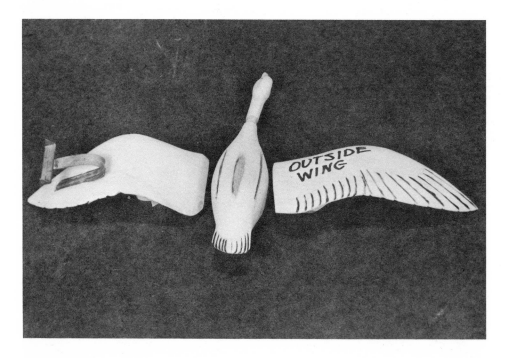

PLATE 27. Flying Canada goose. Wing feathers and tail feathers carved. Note slots in body for mounting wings. (Note: The shallow cuts for wing and tail feathers have been blacked in on the model to aid in showing shape and location.)

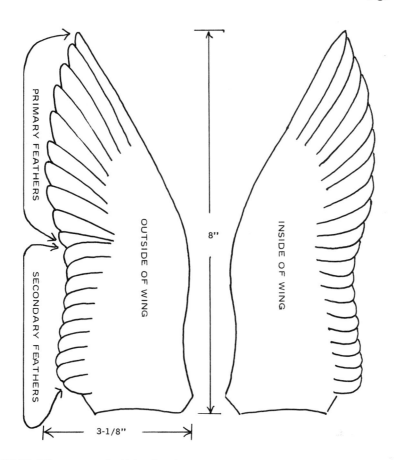

FIGURE 30. Wing patterns for flying Canada geese.

Put some Elmer's glue on the wing edge, and also on the inside edges of the body cut. Insert the wings, and if they need be adjusted a little one way or another, do it now, because when the glue hardens you will not be able to move them.

Put some Plastic Wood or Wood Dough at the joints where the wings and body meet. After this has hardened, it can be trimmed and sanded smooth. It helps to smooth out the lines where wings and body intersect. A small half-round riffler, or wood file, can be used to smooth the Plastic Wood before sanding. A common, coarse rat-tail file can be used if you do not have the riffler.

When you put the Plastic Wood or Wood Dough around the base of the wings, press it firmly with the fingers, to force out any air pockets.

Eyes, Legs and Feet

*T*he bird you are making will need eyes. I nearly always use glass eyes that I buy from a taxidermist supply company. I buy crystal clear eyes, with black pupils, and I paint the iris color on the back side of the eye. If water color paint is used for this purpose, the cement you stick the eye in the head with won't lift off or absorb the color, as it would do if you used regular oil paint.

A friend who makes birds once told me that when he needed eyes, he would buy a string of cheap pearl beads. Each string would have many sizes that could be matched in pairs. These beads were cemented in holes drilled in the bird's head, and then were painted on the outside. After the paint dries, a drop of shellac or varnish on the eye makes it look lifelike.

Another way to make an eye is to collect several sized nail sets—the tool used by carpenters to set nails into wood so that the head won't show. Mark the spot on each side of the bird's head where the eye should be. By pressing the right sized nail set against the spot marked, and twisting at the same time, you will find the indentation very similar in shape to a glass eye. Don't make the indentation too deep.

Paint the whole eye the iris color, and when dry, paint on a spot of black for the pupil. Later, coat it with a little shellac or clear varnish. When the varnish is dry, you will have a hard time distinguishing it from a glass eye.

Setting Eyes

Setting a pair of glass eyes in a bird's head is very important. You can ruin a perfectly good carving by setting the eyes in the wrong position.

Select the correct spot for the eye. Drill a hole larger than you normally would for the conventional glass eye. Select the proper eye, which should be larger than those ordinarily used, since you are going to bring the upper and lower lid out over the glass eye.

Fill the hole with Duratite white surfacing putty. Insert the glass eye,

72

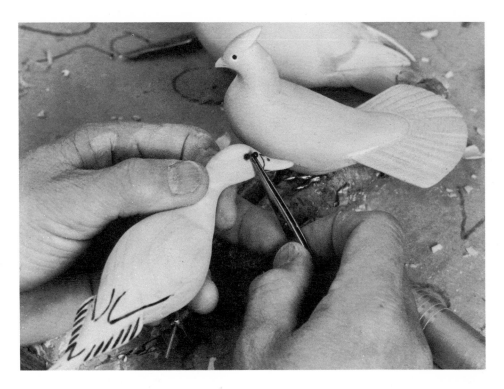

PLATE 28. Glass eye being set in duck's head. Bird in background has a completed eye.

letting the putty squeeze out around it. Work this putty over the glass and add more putty at the top—no harm to cover the eye completely. Don't try to smooth this putty when soft. Let it harden—overnight is best. Now, with a sharp knife, cut the shape of the eye desired. Make it a bit oval shaped instead of round. File or cut the top lid to shape and sand smooth, being careful not to touch the glass with sandpaper which will scratch it. The sharp knife will not scratch. The same idea works well on hawks and eagles, the only difference being that their eyes are set deeper and at an angle. This deep set eye with a heavy top lid gives hawks a fierce look.

Duratite surfacing putty is quick setting, sticks to almost any surface, and does not shrink. It is sold at most hardware stores. If not available, Plaster of Paris could be used, but is not as durable. I have used DAP which is a paste form of patching plaster and comes already mixed in a can. It dries slower than surfacing putty, though not as hard. It needs to be a putty type compound that will stick to wood and glass and will not shrink. DAP and surfacing putty are made by the same company: DAP, Inc. The surfacing putty is waterproof which is an asset.

Legs

The bird now needs two legs. These legs I make of wire, or fine copper tubing. I prefer brass wire to galvanized or steel, because solder sticks to it better. Steel and galvanized wire is stiffer than brass, and is all right to use. You can buy small coils of galvanized wire at most hardware stores. For a medium size bird such as a robin, a wire coat hanger will make good legs. Cut the wire to the desired length, and clean it well with sandpaper. If there is black paint on the wire coat hanger, sand it off.

For chickadees, you will need No. 52 wire. Most coat hangers are either No. 42 or No. 45 wire, and are the right size for a heron that stands about 10 inches high. For ducks about 8 inches long, I use manganese bronze welding rod, size No. 30. The bronze welding rod is quite hard, but can be cut with heavy cutting pliers, or a file.

You need drills the size of each of these wires you intend to use. On the larger drills you can use an electric drill, or large size pin vise. This large

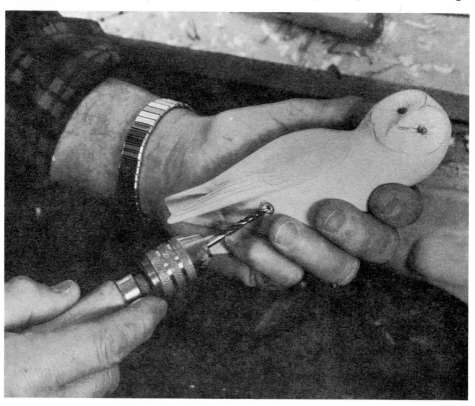

PLATE 29. Drilling leg holes with large size hand pin vise.

size pin vise has a wood handle and takes drills No. 1 to No. 60.

Drilling with the hand vise is slower, but more accurate. Very often I use these drills in the slow turning rotary tool, which I described earlier.

Mark the spot where the leg wires intersect the body, and with the correct size drill make a hole at the angle you wish to set the leg. Drill into the body about half way through, or the length of the drill, whichever comes first. Cut off two pieces of wire slightly longer than you will need. Straighten these wires with a pair of pliers. File one end of each wire to a point. Insert this pointed end into the hole drilled, and push it in with the pliers until it is firm. Bend the protruding leg wires to the desired angle. Bend again where the feet will be placed.

Check the length of the leg by comparing it with the picture, or whatever model you are using. Make a little file mark where the foot will be. This will help when mounting the bird on its base.

Feet

I prefer to make the feet from sheet lead. Most feet can be made from the same thin flashing lead used in making wing patterns. For a small bird like a chickadee, take a piece of lead about 1¼″ x ¼″. Drill a hole the size of the leg wire in the center. With a pair of small, sharp scissors cut out the three toes and heel.

Spread the toes apart, and smooth edges by scraping with a knife blade. Make two of these, a right and a left. The short toe will be on the inside. If you plan to solder the lead to the wire, then scrape the lead clean around the top side of the hole.

For the feet of a small duck, cut out a triangular piece of lead approximately the size of the foot, with a small pair of pointed pliers. You may have to grind them to a point. Grab the lead with the pliers, and with a small hammer tap the jaws together on an anvil or other metal surface. This will make the webb on one side. Do the same thing on the other side. Drill a hole for the leg wire, and trim the foot to shape.

A duck the size of a mallard should have a foot made a bit differently. On a block of very hard wood (I use white holly), carve three round grooves in a triangle. The same angle is used as for the toes of the foot. Carve these grooves about 1/8 inch wide and 1/8 inch deep. Drill a hole at the base of the three toes. These grooves are to raise the shape of the toes of the lead foot.

Place a large sized triangular piece of lead over the grooves. Pin it there with a nail driven through the leg wire hole. Lay a small ice pick on the flat lead above the groove, and tap the lead into the groove with a hammer. Do this on all three grooves separately. Remove the lead and turn it over. You should have a foot like this with raised toes.

You will need to trim the edges of the foot and the webb. Use scissors, a knife, or a file. It may be necessary to practice making this foot a few times.

If you decide to make an osprey, or a large eagle, say 12 to 18 inches body length, the feet on these birds of prey present quite a problem. I used to cut them out of a piece of heavy lead (8 lb. per sq. ft.) and file them to shape, but it was difficult to make the claws, and they were soft and bent out of shape easily. So, I worked out another method that requires some soldering. It takes one about four hours to make a pair of feet by this method.

From a plumbing shop, get a scrap piece of 8 lb. lead pipe 4 inches in

PLATE 30. Method of forming duck's foot.

diameter. Split and flatten it out. Cut out the pattern of the foot the same as for the chickadees, but of course wider.

Build up the space between wood leg and lower leg with fibreglass cement. After it sets up it can be filed and sanded to a smooth finish.

With all the new cements and epoxies on the market, you can use these instead of solder, in most instances. I prefer to use solder, as I have been using it for years and am used to working with it.

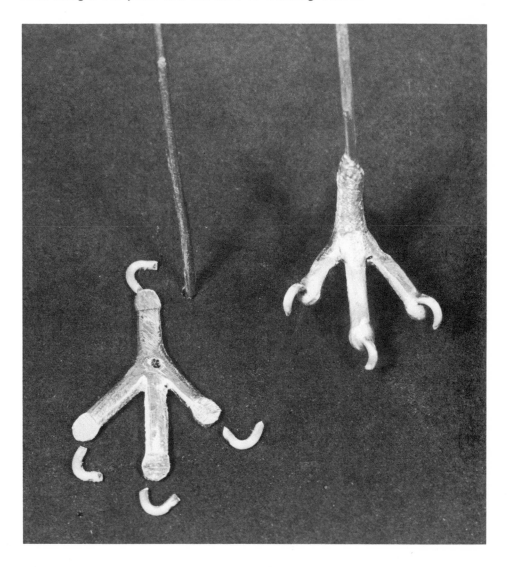

PLATE 31. Osprey foot parts and assembled foot.

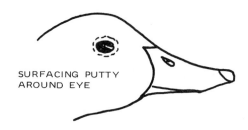

SURFACING PUTTY
AROUND EYE

FIGURE 31. Setting an eye. Fill around eye with surfacing putty.

Casting Feet

Another method of making lead feet for birds is to cast them in a carved, wooden mold. Use a block of hardwood (maple preferred). Mark out the size foot you want in the middle of the block quite near the top with the heel or rear toe up.

Carve the shape of the foot in the wood. You should carve any joints or ridges you want on the toes. If you are making a web foot, carve out the space between the toes for the web and make a few indentations in the wood with the edge of a file or rasp by hitting the edge with a hammer. These rough marks will show up on the casting and make the web look realistic. Cut a groove from the rear toe or heel up to the top of the block and enlarge it like a funnel. You will pour the molten lead into the mold through this funnel shaped opening.

Now fit a flat block of wood on the face of the carved block. This block of wood can be thinner than the carved block. It's only function is to hold the molten lead in the mold.

Place the two blocks together and clamp them tight, either in a hand clamp or vise jaws, pouring funnel up. Now you have the mold ready to pour. The first pouring may not bring out a perfect foot but the second should.

The mold works best after it has been charred. If the casting is too thin or uneven in a certain spot, work the mold over to remedy this. After a few tries, you should have no trouble.

I melt lead in a small plumber's ladle over a small propane gas torch and pour it into the mold with a teaspoon. The lead must be hot enough to pour well but not hot enough to burn the mold. *Never* pour hot lead into a wet or damp mold.

For casting lead feet get some discarded lead wheel weights from a garage or filling station. These weights are used to balance the wheels and tires of automobiles. After use, they are usually discarded or sold for junk. The weights are a little too hard in their regular state so mix a little soft lead with them when melting—just enough to make them bendable without breaking. Pour this molten metal in the wood forms for all types of feet.

Small pieces of sheet lead can be cut up and placed in the ladle. *Note: Never put a piece of wet or cold lead into the hot molten metal.* It will fly and you could get a bad burn. *Be sure to handle this hot lead carefully.*

If you do not have an iron ladle or pot to melt the lead in, you can use a heavy steel mixing spoon. Also one of those small black cast iron kettles that are sold in department stores for use as ash trays could be used. Be sure it is a good solid one.

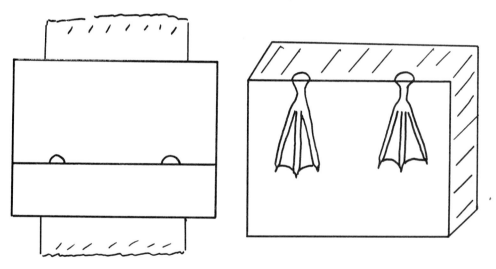

FIGURE 32. Form for pouring lead feet.

In making molds for feet, a right and left should be carved. They can be carved side by side and both poured at one time.

For cutting the toe grooves for small birds, a dentist's round burr (get a used one from your dentist) used in the Foredom flexible shaft tool is excellent. Larger toe grooves can be made with a gouge. Carve feet on both sides of the block and use two of the thinner face blocks and you can pour four feet at one time. The legs can be built up with the same method as mentioned for feet cut out or hammered to shape.

Plastic Auto Body Putty

If you do not have facilities for soldering, or have never used solder, there is a fiberglass compound that can be molded to almost any desired shape. This plastic body putty is used by automobile repair shops for filling in dents in car bodies. It will adhere to both wood or metal, dries hard in about twenty minutes, and can be cut or sanded. Shrinkage is almost nothing, and it is as strong, if not stronger, than the pieces you are bonding. You mix it with a few drops of a liquid hardener that comes separate from the plastic material. Mix only what you plan to use at the time. It sticks best to raw woods, and clean metal. Don't try to use it over painted surfaces.

It is perfect for setting wings, building up V cuts, and covering wire legs to give them texture and make them more natural looking. It is quite sticky, and takes a bit of doing to get it shaped properly. The best thing to do is to build it thicker than needed and then file or sand it to shape after it hardens.

Mallard drakes have two small curled-up feathers on the tail which are a most attractive feature. These can be shaped from lead much more effectively than they can be carved and the results are much more practical. Drill a hole and insert the two lead "feathers" after they have been cut out and bent to shape. On small models, tin will work well. Cement them in place using white glue or other strong cement.

Bases for Mounting

*I*f you are using a piece of driftwood as a base on which to mount the bird, you can saw the piece so that it will set flat on a table or shelf, or mount it on a pine board base which has been leveled off. The reason I mention pine boards is because they are easy to obtain. Pine can be worked easily, and will not warp out of shape as much as some of the other woods. You can purchase pine boards at nearly all lumber yards, although I tried in Florida to get pine and had to settle for Minnesota spruce. It was harder to cut and had several solid knots.

Many pieces of driftwood, even though they are excellent for bases, will not stand without being fastened to a flat wood base.

Decide just how you want the piece of driftwood to set. Saw the bottom square across. Set it on a board and draw around it. Draw the shape you wish for the base. Saw it out on a band saw and bevel the edges. Drill two holes through the base, and countersink these holes on the bottom side to make a place for the screw heads. With a small gouge make uneven gouge cuts, with the grain of the wood, over all the exposed top of the wood base. Leave the space where the driftwood sets smooth. Insert two flathead wood screws, about No. 10 x 1¼″, up through the holes in the base and into the driftwood. This should hold it firm on the base.

Stain the base with flat raw umber mixed with turpentine. I prefer to saw the driftwood so that the saw cuts do not show. If there is a long projection that must be removed, break it off, or saw it and rough up the remaining part with a coarse rasp. A little stain, the color of the driftwood, will help camouflage the cut.

You can make a good flat base by cutting an oval block from a pine board. Mark out the oval the desired size, saw it out, then bevel the edges and sand smooth. Paint it to resemble a sand beach, or mound of earth.

You can also use a thicker piece of wood, and saw and rasp out a piece that resembles a rock, and paint it similar to one.

Rocks are especially good for ducks and geese, while flat oval pieces are fine for shore birds, such as sandpipers.

81

If you want a very natural looking base on which to mount ducks or geese, saw out an irregular oval from a flat piece of one inch board. Bevel off the edges with a hatchet, knife, or rasp. Leave this base quite rough, and better still, rough up any smooth places so the glue you will be putting on it will adhere well. If you wish to have one bird higher than the other, in case you have a pair, cut out a small, irregular block to the shape of a flat rock. Screw this to the flat base near one end. It is better to insert the screws in the bottom of the base and let them come up through and into the block. Paint the complete base with raw umber, gray, or any good earthy color using flat paint. After the paint is dry, cover the entire top with Elmer's or any white glue. Spread it on thick with a brush, then set it on a large piece of cardboard and cover it with sand, pressing the sand into the glue. Let it dry for three or four hours, or even longer, then dump off the excess sand, and with a soft brush clean off all pieces that didn't stick to the base.

PLATE 32. Pintails mounted on driftwood base.

If your sand is a good color to suit the purpose, fine, but if not, paint the sand to any desired color. The better way to paint the sand is with an air brush, or spray gun, but you can put the paint on with a regular hair brush if you mix the paint thin. Use flat paint.

When I do not have regular sand from a lake or sea shore, I buy a package of parakeet gravel, and use that. This gravel is white, but can be painted to any color. To make it look like snow, use white paint on the base first coat, and cover with the white parakeet gravel. The reason for painting the bare wood of the base is in case the sand doesn't stick completely all over, the paint will show through and not be noticed, whereas, if you glued the gravel to the bare wood base, the wood shows through and spoils the effect.

You can do the same thing (as outlined above) and coat only the base with sand, but paint the block to resemble a rock. A small piece of

PLATE 33. Eagle with duck, mounted on driftwood base. Eagle with raised wings (right) mounted on combination driftwood and painted wood block.

driftwood can be used instead of the block. Coating a base with sand is a simple operation and whether you paint the sand or leave it natural, it makes a most effective mounting especially for shore birds.

If you use this type of base, I would suggest that felt be glued to the underside. This is to keep any pieces of sand near the edge from scratching the furniture upon which it might be placed.

By using different colored sand, very attractive and realistic bases can be made. If you wish, add a few small rocks here and there.

For cormorants and gulls, a good base can be made to resemble an ocean buoy. Whittle out a round stick, about 2 inches at the base, and 8 inches long. Taper from the base to about 1¼ inches at the top. Sand it fairly smooth and mount it on an oval block. Have it leaning at an angle, as it does in the ocean. Paint the buoy red or black, and the base blue-green to resemble water. Put a white number on the buoy about one half the way up from the base. Remember the red buoys have even numbers, and the black buoys odd numbers. Off the harbor where I live there is a black one marked No. 7, and I have copied it many times.

On the driftwood bases, try to get flat pieces for ducks and shore birds. The higher pieces are better for herons and song birds.

Mounting Birds on Bases

I prefer to mount the bird on its permanent base before the bird is painted. By doing it this way you can make adjustments without spoiling the paint job. I mount the bird so that it is removable.

Insert the leg wires in the bird's body, and cut and bend them to the desired angles. Pick out a suitable base of driftwood, or whatever you plan to mount the bird on. Mark the two spots where the feet will rest, and drill the holes to accommodate the leg wires. Drill these holes one size larger than the size of leg wire. Slide the lead feet over the leg wires, and insert legs into holes drilled in the base. Set legs at correct height, and position the feet. Solder the foot to the leg wire, or use some epoxy glue. I always use solder, but if I were using glue or cement, I would place a piece of paper under the foot so that the glue wouldn't stick to the base. I would lay the paper on the base, and push the leg wires down through it. This will keep any glue from getting in around the leg wire, and the drilled hole. After the solder has cooled or the cement hardened and you are sure you have set the bird in the right pose, remove the bird from the base. It is now ready for priming, setting the eyes, and then painting. After the bird is painted, you know you have a base ready for it and that it will fit.

PLATE 34. Buoy No. 7 with sea gull.

Many spread-winged, or flying birds, look well just hanging on the wall. A wall hanger of some sort must be used. I made a hanger several years ago that has worked out exceptionally well. All that is needed to hang it on is a nail driven in the wall. It can be made from 24 gauge galvanized or plain steel. You can get this from any sheet metal shop.

The wing nearest to the wall, to which the hanger is to be attached, should be made thicker than the outside wing. This will allow more wood for cutting a groove to insert the hanger.

Make the slot a real tight fit, and slide the hanger into the slot. Fasten into place with strong glue. The hanger can be bent so the bird will hang in any desired position. This plan is for a wing that lies nearly flat against the wall, but it can be used from the wing tip in the event both wings are up.

The size and weight of the bird determines the thickness of the steel for the hanger. For a goose about 9 inches long, I would use 24 gauge. A smaller bird, say 4 inches long, could be held with 26 gauge. A larger one might need 20, or perhaps 18 gauge. The points on the hanger keep the bird from tipping endwise.

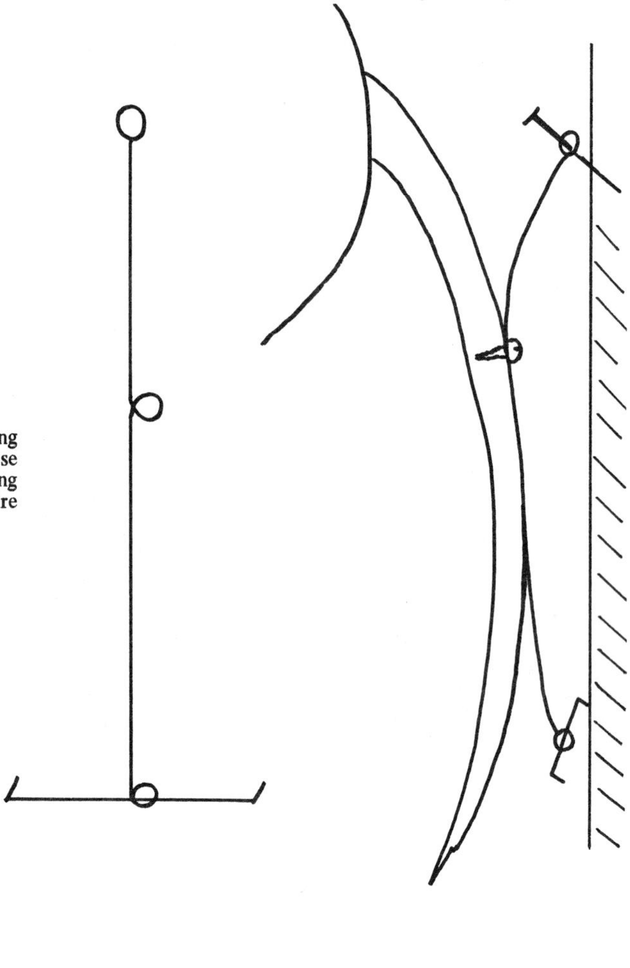

FIGURE 33. Method of mounting a flying bird to the wall by use of a wire hanger. Variation using sheet metal in the place of wire is shown in Plate 35.

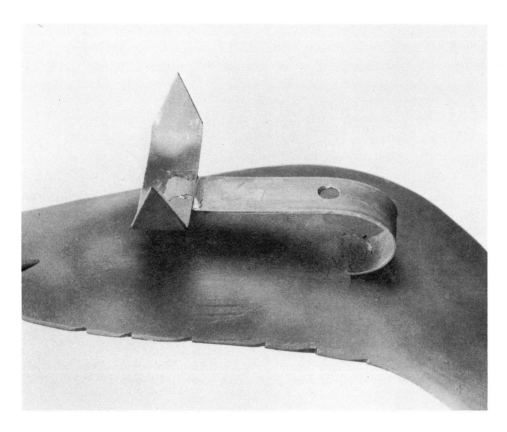

PLATE 35. Wall hanger on finished bird (close-up of back side of wing).

Metal Stamps

There are several ways of marking your carvings. Your name can be painted on, burned in with an electric pencil, carved in or stamped with a metal stamp. Henry Evers Company, Inc., 72 Oxford Street, Providence, Rhode Island, 02905 makes a small, inexpensive metal stamp that can be used for marking either wood or soft metal. They also will make up any type stamp that you might wish. Place the letters against the wood and hit with one quick blow of a hammer. Your name is there permanently.

Painting

$\mathcal{N}$ow that the bird is sanded and mounted on a permanent base, the next step is to paint it. In this chapter I will try to give step-by-step procedures for painting birds in general, as well as detailed instructions on how to paint some of the more common birds.

New wood should be primed with some type of primer-sealer. Priming fills the pores of the wood, and makes a suitable base on which to complete the detailed feather painting. There are many excellent primers on the market, and I have tried several of them, but the one I prefer for priming a newly carved bird is Gesso. It can be purchased at any art store, and makes a good primer for both oil and water color paints. Just paint it on the raw wood with a brush that has been wet in plain water. After it is dry, sand it down and the bird is ready for final paint. Do not use it to prime the metal feet of the bird, and be sure there is no oil on the wood. Gesso will not stick to an oily surface.

The primed bird should be sanded lightly with fine sandcloth or paper. A partially worn piece which has been used while making the bird is just the thing. It is worn down some and will produce a smoother surface. This way you are able to make a piece of sandpaper work twice.

The time to insert the glass eyes is just after you have done this light sanding. If you set them before this, you are very apt to scratch the glass with the sandpaper or sandcloth. Mark the spot where each eye is to be placed and make sure they are evenly matched on both sides of the head. An otherwise good job of carving and painting a bird can be quickly ruined if the eyes are not set properly. Drill a small hole with a hand drill, then enlarge this hole to fit the eye by using a small tapered reamer.

Glass eyes are made by hand by inserting ends of wire into molten glass; thus when you buy a pair of eyes, they will be joined by a short piece of soft steel wire. After selecting the proper size and color of eye, snip the wire, leaving about 1/8 inch extending from the glass. This wire helps steer

PLATE 1.　Author holding a Canada goose coming in for a landing.

PLATE 2.　Miniature owls, approximately one-half life-size. (left to right) Screech owl, gray phase, saw whet owl, and screech owl, red phase.

PLATE 3. Old squaw drake decorative decoy, life-size.

PLATE 4. Group of Canada geese carved one-third size.

90

PLATE 5. Group of pintails carved approximately one-half size.

PLATE 6. Decorative black duck decoy, life-size, courtesy of Robert Kurtz. The spotted sandpiper is also life-size.

91

PLATE 7. Wood ducks, life-size.

the eye when inserting it. Fill the eye hole with Duratite surfacing putty, or any good seam filler such as DAP Spackling Compound. Press the glass eyes into the sockets, set them evenly, and let them protrude about one-quarter of their thickness. Clean and smooth off any excess putty that may have oozed out around the eye. Eyes may also be set with Plastic Wood or plain white glue. Surfacing putty is my choice because it hardens quickly and does not shrink.

There is no need to be too fussy about the first primer coat on the bird, but the entire surface of the wood should be well covered with paint. If the bird is white, two or more primer coats may be necessary. Make sure that the primer coat is completely dry before attempting to do the finish painting. If you try to paint over it too soon, the first coat will soften and brush off, leaving a bare spot.

The finish coat may be done with either regular artist's oils, or with acrylics. You may want to try both to determine which suits you best. Just remember that you can paint over acrylics with oils, but you cannot paint over oils with acrylics. I will explain how I paint with oils and will also give some helpful hints on the use of acrylics in another section of this chapter.

It is very difficult to explain exactly how to paint a bird and describe just what color of paint goes where. A good color picture makes an excellent guide. I prefer to use a mounted bird or a study skin, instead of the picture, but you may be making birds for which you just can't get study skins. In this case there is no better guide than a good painting or print by a reputable artist, or a good closeup color photograph. A live bird would be ideal, but few of us live near enough to an aviary, or have the facilities for keeping live birds.

When painting with oils, mix the colors on a palette, and apply the undercoat colors as you see them in the picture or on the model. Leave the feathering until later. Keep away from distinct, sharp lines where colors meet. Blend these colors for a softer line by stippling with a dry brush, hitting the darker color very lightly with the ends of the brush and working the dark color into the light one. There are times, of course, when distinct, sharp lines are necessary and desirable.

Painting with oil colors over the flat colors should produce a finish, not flat and not glossy, but rather with just a little sheen. A bird in real life is not shiny, but its feathers do have a soft sheen. To get this sheen finish, I experimented for several years with all types of paints and methods of

PLATE 36. Method of holding brush to stipple, using left hand as support. Uneven block used as a rest to steady brush hand.

application. Apparently the flat paint absorbs the oil in the regular oil color with the result that is to be desired.

The head of a mallard drake has a green tinge that looks like bronze powder. This is called iridescence and is seen in the feathers of many birds. I have used green bronze powders which look good for a time, but eventually it will fade and turn yellow when exposed to sunlight. I therefore paint the entire head a medium green; then go over the top of the head, the line through the eye, and under the throat, with black. Using a soft, short, sable brush, I lightly stipple the black into the green. This has to be done very carefully in order to maintain a predominance of green on the high spots.

I seldom wait for the oil colors to dry before painting over them. Painting in a wet state blends the colors better, and looks more natural. In painting pictures, most artists have a brush for each color, but in painting a bird you can use the same brush for all colors if you wish. Just make sure to wash out the brush between colors. I still use a separate white brush.

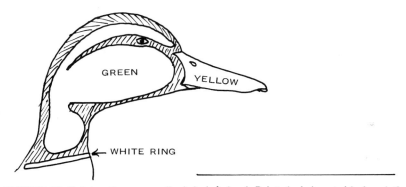

FIGURE 34. Paint pattern on mallard drake's head. Paint shaded parts black and the balance green.

Brush Washer

To make a brush washer, take a widemouthed glass jar, similar to a peanut butter jar, and fit the bottom with a screen. To make the screen, take a piece of metal window screening and cut out a circle (with a pair of tin shears) about 3/4 inches larger around than the inside of the jar. With a pair of flat nose pliers, bend the outside edge of the screen down at right angles making it just small enough to fit inside the jar. If the screen has a tendency to crimp when bending, just cut a few V slots around the rim. Place the screen, with the bent part down, in the bottom of the jar. The flat part of the screen will sit up off the bottom. The space under the screen will hold the paint settlings so that you won't stir up the color every time you wash a brush. Fill the jar two-thirds full of turpentine, or better still, a similar paint thinner called Pine Thinner. It is not as sticky as turpentine and costs less. When washing brushes in the thinner, don't rub the bristles too hard on the screen, or it will wear them out. Wipe off all the paint you can from the brush with a rag before dipping it in the washer.

Always clean every brush when you are through painting. Never let the paint set in the bristles overnight. A little vaseline rubbed into the bristles which are shaped between the thumb and forefinger, will keep the brush in good condition. Before using, a few shakes in the brush cleaner jar next morning, will dissolve the vaseline.

Brushes

Sable hair brushes are best for painting birds. You will need some flats, or brights, and a few rounds in various sizes. Start with three or four brushes, and then buy the ones which best suit you. A good brush for long, fine lines is a show-card writer's lettering brush in size No. 1 or 2. It has long hairs and will make a straighter line than a short hair brush, especially if your hand is not steady. It cleans easily, and with proper care will last a long time. I have used one such brush a full year, and it is still good.

How to Hold Birds While Painting

When you started to paint this bird, you no doubt wondered how to hold it so that both hands would be free for painting. There are several methods. One is the use of an engraver's ball, with a small hand vise clamped in it, and the bird's feet clamped in the hand vise. The engraver's ball can be moved in almost any position and will stay in place. It is the best holder I have ever tried, but only a few of us are fortunate enough to own one. The one I have was given to me by a friend whose father was a silversmith.

Another type of clamp that is very effective can be easily made. Purchase a small hand vise from a hardware store and remove the wooden handle. Be sure to save the handle for later use on a home-made knife. Cut out a round, flat block of wood about 8 inches in diameter by 2 inches thick. This can be made of any type wood you might happen to have on hand. Drill about eight or ten holes in the face of the block at different angles. The size of the holes should be the same as the size of the shank on the hand vise to assure a smooth fit. By clamping the bird's legs in the vise jaws, and inserting the vise shank in the different holes, you can angle the bird and turn the vise to get almost any desired position.

PLATE 37. Mallard drake clamped in engraver's ball for painting.

PLATE 38. Mallard hen clamped in hand vise, with handle removed, held by drilled round block.

Feather Painting

When I paint a white bird, such as a sea gull, I always give it two coats of flat white before putting on the final coat of titanium white. In oil color, I prefer titanium to zinc or flake white.

In painting the final coat on a sea gull it is best to let the gray color dry; then paint the white breast and sides, and feather the sides over the gray. This eliminates smudging the white.

When painting the feet be careful not to flick the brush. It can cause little spatters of paint to fly on the body.

When painting the sides of a mallard, pintail, or similar duck with fine feathering, I paint on the light gray first, and then, with a very fine and Pointed brush, make the little uneven feather marks. Before the paint dries, I stipple it with a large, soft brush to even out the lines so that one won't be more pronounced than another.

PLATE 39. Mallard hen showing painted feather detail.

In painting the speculum, or blue feathers on a mallard's wing, paint them first with ultramarine blue and then highlight with a little blue bronze powder. This will liven it up a bit.

Perhaps the best way to paint a bird is to begin at the tail, and paint the feathers, working toward the head. It is much like shingling the roof of a house. Short brush strokes are preferred to long ones. For painting fine lines, I like a Delta signwriter's brush No. 1, style 125. Sometimes, a faint outline in a darker or lighter color around a feather will make it look more natural.

One method of painting a bird is to brush on all the base colors first with a wide brush. A good brush for large surfaces is a Grumbacher No. 4614 Oxhair. They come in ¼, ½, and ¾ inch widths. It is a flat brush with a short handle. Blend the colors together where necessary. Next, with a small and pointed brush, draw the feather lines in the proper colors. Before the paint dries, brush over these feather lines with a very soft bristle brush. Have the brush dry and barely touch the paint with the tips of the bristles. Make the strokes from tail to head. This will soften the texture and blend the feathers. Sometimes the paint will dry faster than you can work it. In such a case, paint a few feathers, then blend and keep on in this manner until finished. If you paint and blend three feathers on one side, do the same three on the other side. If you were to paint one side today, and leave the other side until tomorrow, the paint would dry and the two sides would look different. Thus the reason for doing the same thing on each side as fast as you progress. I usually paint a bird in stages, since I am often interrupted. I paint the bird's back first, in base color, then outline the feathers and blend with a dry brush. The breast and underparts can be done later and feathered where they join at the sides. The head can be done separately, then the bill. The feet should be left until last, otherwise in handling them you may rub off the paint in places. In painting the feet, the web between the toes is usually darker than the toes. The inside toe has two bones with one joint; the middle three, with two joints; and the outside four, with three joints.

An uneven block of wood is good for holding the brush hand steady. At times I use my left hand as a support for my right hand which holds the brush.

Painting a bird in three dimensions is quite different from painting on a flat canvas. To get the right position is hard at times, and you may find yourself standing almost on your head to get at some out-of-the-way spot. The engraver's ball with the vise, or the block of wood with the holes

PLATE 8.   Near life-size eagle. Southwest Harbor is in the background.

PLATE 9. Wilson Snipe, approximately two-thirds life-size.

102

PLATE 10. Cardinals.

PLATE 11. Ringneck pheasants, one-fourth life-size.

PLATE 12. Eiders recently completed by the author.

104

drilled at angles to hold the vise, is a great help on just such an occasion. You can swivel the subject into almost any desired position. When painting a chickadee, in order to paint the underpart of the tail, I always remove the bird from the ball, or block, and hold it upside down with my left hand while I paint the feathers with the brush in my right hand. When doing this, steady the left hand against the table edge or something else solid.

One way to paint the head and cheeks of a black duck is to paint the entire head dark, the color of the darker feathers. Let this color dry well. Paint the entire head the color of the lighter feathers. Before this light color dries, using a pointed instrument such as an old fashioned pen, a scratch awl, or sharpened wire, make the fine feather lines by scratching through the light color to expose the hidden, dark undercoat. After each stroke wipe clean the tool you are using to make the scratches.

When painting lighter colored feather lines over a dark-bodied bird, use quick drying colors instead of regular oil colors. A dark body color, such as raw umber or black oil paints will partly absorb any light oil color painted over it. By using quick drying colors in place of oils for the dark color this absorption of the light color is prevented.

For painting the bird's metal feet, I use a standard metal primer. You can find a small spray can of gray automobile body primer at a hardware or automotive store. It is quick drying and takes paint for the finish coat very well.

Painting with Acrylics

Many carvers are allergic to oil paints, turpentine, and paint thinners. For these persons, and many others who wish to use quick drying paint with a water base, the new acrylic paints are now available. This type of paint has many advantages. Any color can be put on over another color without blending. You can paint yellow over blue or even white over red. Due to its quick drying characteristics, it is difficult to blend one color with another on the feathers the way you can with oils. This is the greatest disadvantage I find in using acrylics. Grumbacher makes a medium called Hyslo that can be mixed with the colors to slow the drying time to as long as six hours. This will hold the paint wet and give the artist time to blend the feathers if he so desires.

Acrylic paint dries almost as it leaves the brush. Brushes must be kept wet or they will harden.

PLATE 40. Life-size pileated woodpecker.

PLATE 41. Life-size willet.

There are gloss mediums and matte mediums, but the finish obtained with the paint as it comes from the jar or tube has about the desired finish. Any of the top-rated brands of acrylics should perform satisfactorily.

Remember that acrylics should be painted over a Gesso base—never over oils or an oily surface. Oils may be used over acrylics however, and this lends lots of possibilities for experimenting. One method of combining the two types of paint would be to prime the bird with Gesso, sand smooth, and then paint the base coat and feather markings with acrylics. Now, with a fine brush and regular oil paints, go over the feathers and feather lines. Before the oil sets, blend with a dry brush.

When using acrylics straight from the tube or jar for feathering a bird, it is necessary to do each feather outline with a small pointed brush being careful to make a series of many small lines with as dry a brush as possible.

Another effective way in which to use acrylics is to use water-thinned paint in light washes, one over the other. Paint in the feather lines first.

I find that this type of paint works very well in an air brush. Just thin with water and clean the brush with water.

If you have never used acrylics, it would be wise to obtain a book on acrylic painting and study it. A small manual comes with the kit for beginners from Grumbacher. There are five colors in the kit which can be mixed to make other colors, but one should also obtain some of the more frequently used browns, greens, and reds to save mixing time. They come in tubes or jars—either is fine. Close the jars and cap the tubes when not in use.

It is possible to paint a bird with acrylics and in five minutes be able to put it in your pocket and walk off. It will dry just that fast. This makes acrylic paint ideal when you want the bird to dry in a hurry.

The Air Brush

In recent years I have used an air brush to some extent. It is a miniature paint spray gun. After a person learns how to use it, many desirable effects can be obtained that never could be accomplished with a regular sable brush, or, let's say, much easier than with a sable brush. You can spray on sheens and highlights, blend and stipple—in fact do almost anything with this brush. You can even write your name with one.

I have had several air brushes, and the one that seems to suit me best is the Model A, made by Thayer and Chandler, 331 So. Peoria St., Chicago, Illinois. I have both a Model A and a Model B. The Model B is supposed to throw twice as much color, and make nearly as fine a line as the Model A.

PLATE 42. Model A Thayer and Chandler air brush, held beside little Atlas air compressor.

The Model A will throw plenty of color for my needs. The catalogue says that the Model B has color openings large enough to handle oil paint or opaque water color without clogging. The Model A has never clogged with me, and I use oil paint in it constantly. I always clean it immediately after every operation. This prevents the pigments from drying and clogging the color parts.

I am no expert on the use of the air brush, but I have had a lot of fun experimenting, and I will pass on what information I have learned the hard way. You can buy books on the use of these brushes, but I never did. I am thinking strongly, now, of getting one. Air brushes are used mostly with ink and water color, but I have always used oil paint.

To get an air brush, hose, and a compressor to furnish the air for it, runs into quite a lot of money, depending on the kind of compressor you choose. Also, it can be operated on carbonic gas that comes in cylinders.

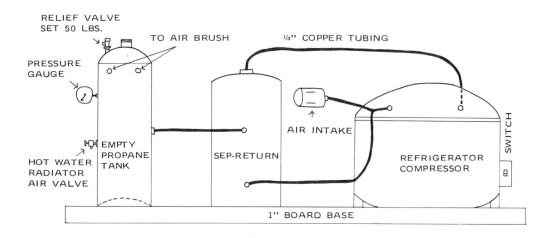

FIGURE 35. Drawing of a quiet compressor.

If you can't have the noise of a compressor running, the gas might be the solution. I never did use the gas, because I always figured the tank would be empty and I would be out of gas just when I needed it most.

The outfit I use is a sort of make-shift affair that I built up, comprised of a ¼ h.p. used electric motor, a small second hand compressor similar to the type used in the earlier electric refrigerators. It is a piston type compressor that has oil in its crankcase. The air tank is a used water pump tank, with an automatic switch that cuts the motor in at 20 lbs. and out at 40 lbs. I use an oil filter in the air line from the tank. This filter has a cotton replaceable element, and is to catch any water or moisture that might collect in the air line. At the end of the air line I have a pressure regulating valve with a needle gauge. With this valve I can control the brush pressure as I desire. I never use over 20 lbs., and if doing fine work, usually drop it down to 10 lbs.

There is on the market a very small motor and air compressor unit. It is inexpensive, and a small air brush with a glass jar comes with it. It is called the Atlas Sprayer, made by K. J. Miller Corporation, Brookfield, Ill. The glass jar air brush that comes with it is okay for painting furniture, but not suitable for the fine work needed for painting birds. If you should purchase one of these units, be sure to order the relief valve that is set to blow off at 20 lbs.; otherwise the unit will build up extra pressure and then blow off the hose.

I have one of these small units that I keep on hand as a spare, and also as a portable unit. They make quite a noise, as the little compressor turns up pretty fast. It is a good, inexpensive outfit for anyone who only uses an air brush off and on. By adding a small tank of about a gallon capacity in the air line, a smoother spray will result.

The makers of the air brushes have automatic compressors that are quiet running, and very elaborate, but as I only use one occasionally, I didn't think the expensive type necessary.

If you would like to try an inexpensive air brush, get a Binks Wren Model A. This is a low priced brush, but it does a fine job when used right. It is not as easy to clean as the conventional type brushes, and for changing colors it is time consuming. I do not care for the small jar that holds the paint, so I improvised an adapter that will let me use one of my regular paint cups.

Should you get an air brush and a compressor, you can have a lot of fun with it.

I mix my colors in paper soufflé cups, the kind used by restaurants for serving relishes and jellies. They are very cheap, if purchased by the carton of 250, and can be discarded.

Take a one inch board three inches wide and about twelve inches long, and bore about eight holes, evenly spaced. These holes should be just large enough for the soufflé cup to fit tightly in at about half way up on the cup.

Squeeze the oil color from the tube into the paper cup. Add some turpentine or paint thinner and stir it up by using a worn-out paint brush. Be sure the brush isn't shedding its hairs. You can mix the paint better with a brush than with a paddle. I find it handy to keep my paint thinner in an oil squirt can.

Mix the colors you wish to use in the paper cups, then pour some of this color into the air brush cup. You should have your air pressure between 10 lbs. and 20 lbs. Before painting the bird directly, try the spray for color and texture on an old piece of newspaper. The paint doesn't have to be mixed as thin as you would expect. It is surprising what thick paint this little brush will handle. For a handle in lifting out the paper soufflé cups and pouring, I use small spring style paper clips.

There are directions that come with the air brush, telling how to set the spray regulator for the different types of spray. The thinner the paint, of course, the greater the spray; but if too thin, it has a tendency to run and not cover well.

You will find this paint spray will be on the bird almost before you can see it, so if you want to get very good results use a large magnifying glass to look through, especially if there is not much contrast between the colors you are using. Using black, or gray and white, you can see it soon enough.

Cleaning the air brush is very simple. Dump the unused paint back into the paper cup. Wipe out the excess paint, and squirt in some paint thinner from the squirt can. With the lever pressed down and pulled back all the way; and holding the air brush in the left hand, cover the nozzle with the fore-finger of the left hand. This will blow the paint back through the cup. Keep doing this several times, adding thinner from the squirt can held in the right hand.

PLATE 43. Method used in cleaning air brush. (Note air pressure gauge at right.) Paper cups hold mixed colors.

To prevent everything getting messed up, spray this into a gallon can. Take an empty gallon turpentine or thinner can, and cut a square hole, say about five inches by five inches, in the wide side. On the bottom of the hole bend out a one inch lip. This is just to catch any drip, so it will run into the can as you clean the brush. Put some masking tape around the edge of this hole to prevent getting cut fingers. Cut the bottom of the hole about three inches from the bottom of the can. This will leave two inches for used thinner to gather. When cleaning the air brush you can hold the front half of it inside the can, and make no mess in the room at all.

Clean your brush after every operation, and never leave it overnight in a dirty condition. It is a precision instrument, and should be cared for as such. A wise practice is never to loan it, either.

When painting over an area, always keep the brush in motion to avoid building up heavy spots of paint. It takes a lot of practice to get the hang of using it, but after you get the technique you will surprise yourself at the things you can do. Don't be discouraged if you goof the first few times. Keep at it.

I will try to explain a few of the operations I use it for.

In painting a male cardinal I paint the entire bird vermilion (Grumbacher), then I mix burnt umber and white, about one-third white, and two-thirds burnt umber. I spray this on the back and tail, and the wing feathers. A little heavier coating is needed on the tail and wings. Then with a hair brush, just wet with turpentine, I outline the feathers. After this dries some, I add the black feather lines, and a little bright red where needed. You can do the same thing with the female bird, but you will be using raw umber over cream or buff color.

A cormorant has a green sheen on its black body. Use a flat, light green paint for this, and spray it on.

Paint the sides of a male mallard gray, and stipple with darker gray. To stipple, drop the air pressure to 10 lbs. and screw in the spray regulator nearly as far as it will go. Try it on the newspaper first, to get the right size spots.

On a wild turkey, spray on the base colors, blending them with the air brush. Then with a fine hair brush paint the feather outlines in black.

In painting a sea gull you are able to get a very white, even color. By spraying the gray first, the white can be brought right to it with a very soft line where the two colors meet.

When painting the underparts of the wings of an osprey, I spray the underside a very light gray, white with a little black and raw umber. After this paint is dry, I lay a template (made of sheet plastic, with holes cut where the dark feathers show) over this wing, and spray all exposed parts with raw umber. Then remove it, and wash in thinner, dry and place it on the other wing for the same process. To hold the template in place on the wing, I use a couple of spring-type clothespins. After removing the template, all the feather markings. show, and can be touched up with a fine hair brush. After this is done, a very light spray of raw umber over the entire gray will soften the texture of the whole thing.

If you paint a bird and it happens to come out a little too light, just mix some of the dark color, and with a very light coat you can darken it to suit yourself. It is so fine a spray that it won't even show.

When you paint a black duck's head by scratching through the light color, the air brush is the proper instrument with which to put on this light color. The air brush is excellent for painting bases, especially the ones that have the sand stuck on the wood base. Almost every day I find something new I can do with my air brush. For instance, the rusty color on a gannett, or the buff on the breast of an American eider. If you want to paint a background, it is swell for doing the clouds. All told, it is a handy little gadget.

Dental Chair Base

I use the base of a dental chair for my painting bench. The dental chair has a double sleeve and will raise and lower to a greater distance than the barber chair. It is raised and lowered by a foot pedal instead of a hand lever. Thus, you can have a larger bench and still operate the chair easily. I built a plywood reinforced table top 48 inches by 32 inches and placed a piece of heavy plate glass over this. The reason for the glass is that it cleans easily. I picked up the glass from a broken store window and had it cut to size for a modest fee. I can paint standing or sitting on a stool, or if I wish I can lower the bench to a position comfortable for sitting in a chair. It is excellent for painting large birds that would be hard to reach from an ordinary height bench. The top height is 39 inches and it will lower to 20 inches. Hang a paper towel holder under one end and you have handy paper towels for cleaning brushes.

PLATE 44. Herring gulls made about 10 years ago. They have been out of doors every summer since.

Remounting on Bases

After the bird has been painted, put it away to dry for a few days in a place where it is warm, but where there will be a minimum of dust. As soon as it is dry place it on the mount that has already been prepared. If you desire it fastened securely, place some Duco cement on the leg wires before inserting them into the drilled holes. I prefer my birds placed so that they may be removed from the base, because I have to ship most of them by parcel post, and it is easier and safer to pack them separately from the mount. I do cement small birds, the size of chickadees, solid to the mount at times.

Go over the bird carefully at this time, and touch up any spots missed during the painting. I always paint right over the glass eyes, then later, with the point of a small, sharp knife, I scrape away this paint from the glass. Be careful not to scratch the eye. If you made the eye with a nailset, or used a bead, it will be necessary to put a drop of clear varnish on it to make it shine.

Decoys

I can remember the time when it was legal to use live ducks as decoys in hunting wildfowl. When hunting black ducks, which probably are the most popular ducks of Maine, we would use a dark mallard hen and a drake. We put the drake in a box and kept it in the blind. The hen was fastened by one of her legs to an anchor line and placed out in the lake in front of the blind. When we saw a flock of ducks overhead, we would poke the drake a little so that he would make a soft quack. The anchored hen would answer him and the flying wild ducks would hear the quacking and very often drop down and light. Almost always they would light outside and swim in, talking all the while with the live decoy. I remember one mallard hen that I had. She was very small and had some white feathers on her back. She was the best caller I ever saw. She could spot a wild duck a mile away and would quack steadily. We never did need a drake to start her calling. The only drawback was the white feathers, we colored them dark brown before each shoot. I really can't remember what we used for dye, probably bacon fat and soot from a burned stick.

The practice of using live decoys was outlawed, which was a good thing.

Even from the time of the Indian, many forms of decoys were used to entice ducks within shooting range. Mounds of clay built up to resemble birds were placed on the beach near the water and crude wood and straw decoys floated in the water. As time advanced, hunters kept trying to make a more realistic decoy in order to fool the waterfowl. Today there are some fantastic birds being produced from wood and paint.

Working decoys must serve two purposes. One is to attract wild birds and bring them within shooting range; another is to please the hunter or the creator of the decoy as he sits and admires them.

I have heard the remark that "beauty is in the eye of the beholder", and no doubt this is true. A block of wood painted black or an old black buoy

117

will decoy the scoters which are not a very wary bird, but few of us would enjoy sitting in a boat or on a ledge looking at a bunch of black buoys out in front of us, so we try to carve decoys that will not only attract the ducks, but will also be pleasing to the eye. However, working decoys don't have to be fancy with a lot of feathers painted on. The general shape and color are most important.

Years ago I decided to go after goldeneye or whistlers as we call them. I didn't have a single decoy, so the evening before I chopped out six blocks with a hatchet, made some rough heads, painted them with quick-drying paint and was off to the ledges before daylight. The paint was still tacky. There was a light snow in the air and I had more birds come to those decoys than I have ever attracted since with better made decoys and many more of them.

It is not an absolute necessity to have a separate set of decoys for each type of duck, but it helps, and the larger the stool the better — particularly with the divers. Sometimes a few decoys are very effective for black ducks who are so wary that the less decoys they have to look over the better. I have had black ducks decoy to scoter models in the early morning hours and quite often eider ducks will come close to scoter decoys. Buffleheads will light to almost any decoy and black duck decoys can be used for scoters with good results. Goldeneyes and bluebills are a lot more choosy. Neither will pay much attention to other decoys and the male goldeneye seems to be

PLATE 45. A pair of mallard working decoys designed by Donal C. O'Brien, Jr., and carved on a carving (multi-carver) machine. They were assembled and painted by the author.

much more wary of decoys than the hens are. One morning when we were hunting goldeneyes and bluebills, we set out about 25 decoys of each type off the point of a ledge with a good space between the two. The birds were thick that day and I can't remember a single bluebill lighting near a golden-eye decoy or a goldeneye lighting near a bluebill decoy.

Twenty five years ago, I decided to make a set of scoter decoys that I could use for black ducks also. Diving ducks always have low tails while blacks and other puddle ducks tend to keep their tails high. Scoters are larger than blacks so I had to compromise. I decided to make a large scoter with a removable head so a black duck head could be attached to the scoter body. The decoys had to be light and easy to transport since many times it was quite a distance from the car to the dock or inland blind. The decoys were made of pine and hollowed out. A 5/8 inch square hole was cut into the neck and a square dowel was inserted. This dowel was made of oak with a

PLATE 46. The Gilley scoter with removable heads.

brass screweye at the bottom for connecting the holding line. By taking the heads out of the decoy, they could be strung on a cordline and the decoy bodies could be strung on a heavier line. It was quite easy to carry a string of six bodies in each hand along with the twelve heads. They were much easier carried and less bulky than if they had had solid bodies. These decoys were quite wide and I have used them for years without a keel on the bottom, but if I were to do it over I might attach a weighted keel. Even in rough water, and that is where most scoters are found, I had little trouble

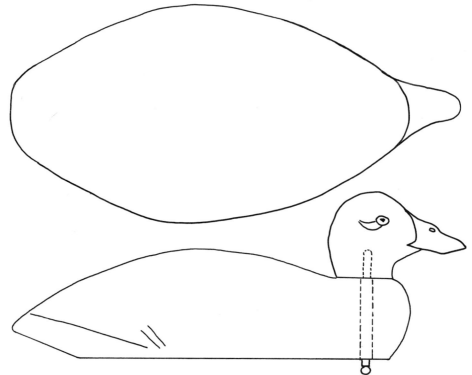

FIGURE 36. White-winged scoter pattern - 17" long.

with these decoys overturning. With a keel they would be even more stable.

These decoys were made from three pieces of wood. A 2 inch thick piece for top and bottom with a middle 1 inch filler. The center was removed from the board and the top and bottom hollowed out with a hand gouge. The block was left solid at the point where the neck square was located. The three pieces were glued together with waterproof glue. The body was then shaped with a drawknife, spokeshave, and rasp. Finally it was rough sanded and ready for paint.

The square hole was drilled for the head with a mortising bit in a drill press. Where the neck and body connected, the spot was made round and all heads carved round at the base. This gives four head positions and any head will fit any decoy. The black duck heads can be used instead of the scoter heads. The idea of this decoy is to provide a set of decoys for two types of birds with only a change of heads. The decoys are fastened to the lead line with a swivel snap hooked into a brass screweye. The square hole through the decoy must be a very loose fit for the square oak dowel that is attached to the head. The brass screweye must be small enough to pass through this body hole also.

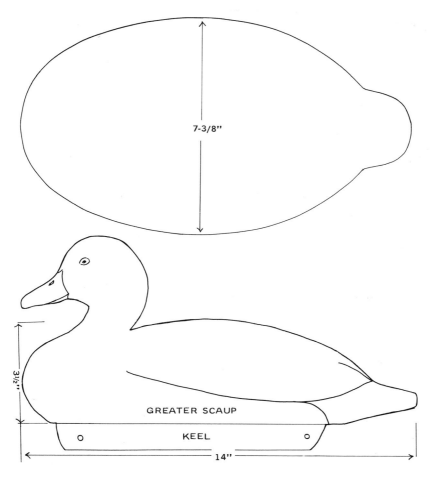

7-3/8"

3½"

GREATER SCAUP

KEEL

14"

FIGURE 37. Scaup decoy pattern - 1/3rd scale.

Now for the more conventional type of working decoy. It can be solid or hollow, and pine or cedar are probably the better woods to use. Decoys are subject to a lot of abuse and these two woods can really take it.

Solid Decoys

For a solid decoy, select a block of solid wood or glue up a block of two or three pieces with waterproof glue. On a piece of cardboard draw a pattern for the profile and of the top view. Square the block and mark out the top view using the pattern. Saw out along these lines with a single cut on each side. You can stop the cut near the end of the tail and back the blade out or saw all the way through, replace these side pieces and fasten to the

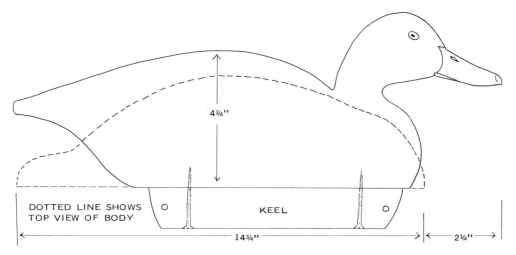

FIGURE 38. Mallard decoy pattern with wooden keel.

center with a small stapler. These staples can be easily removed later. Be sure to place them in a spot that will not be hit by the saw on the next cut. Now you have a square block again, but it is in three pieces. Lay it on its side and transfer the side profile pattern to it. Cut along these lines and the body is ready to be carved.

The bottom is flat and the easiest way to handle this body is to screw a narrow strip of wood about six inches long to the bottom similar to a short keel. This block can be clamped in a vise and a drawknife, rasp, and spokeshave used to shape it. Surform rasps made in flat, half round and round are great for taking off wood fast without gouging. Don't forget a hatchet if you want to remove the excess wood fast, but be very careful. After the body is shaped and smoothed with sandpaper or sand cloth, cut in the feather lines you desire. A good tool for this is a small V tool sometimes called a parting tool.

On a working decoy, it is very wise to keep the wing tips flat down on the body. If you raise them, they are sure to get broken off or a line caught under them.

Saw out a head for this particular bird and carve it to shape. Drill a dowel hole in the head and one in the body. Be sure the head fits the body well. If you use a bit of the exact size of the dowel, the fit will be quite tight. I would recommend sanding down the dowel for a looser fit to give space for the glue. In time to come, the dowel could swell and split the neck if the fit is too tight. No doubt you have seen old decoys where this very thing has happened. You are now ready to balance your decoy.

Before the decoy is painted, you should float it to determine where to put the keel. The keel should be made from oak about 3/4 inch thick, 1½ inches deep and for a large black duck about 11 inches long. Drill a 1/4 inch hole in both ends horizontal to take the anchor line. Drill a screw hole to

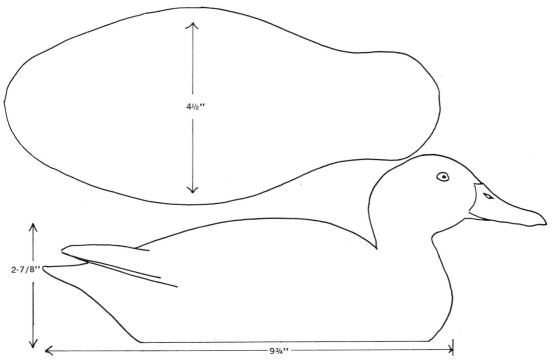

FIGURE 39. Cinnamon teal decoy pattern, approximately ½ size.

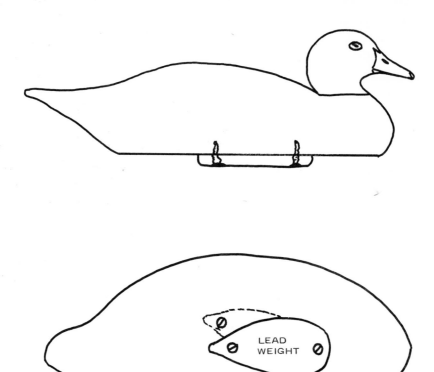

SIMPLE LEAD WEIGHT TO BALANCE DECOY. SHIFT
TO ONE SIDE OR THE OTHER AS NECESSARY.

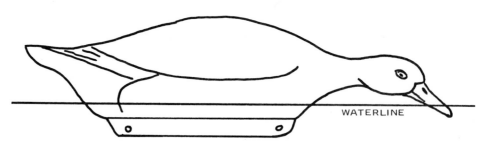

WATERLINE

FIGURE 40. Decoy patterns showing weights and keel.

attach it to the body about 1½ inch in from each end. This hole should be countersunk for the screw head. Place lengthwise on the bottom and fasten in place with brass screws. Never use steel screws because they will rust. Holes can be bored in the keel and filled with lead to make it balance more effectively. The keel will hold the decoy steady in rough water just as the keel on a sailboat does. Caution: Never pour hot lead into a hole drilled in a wet board. Be sure the wood is dry.

If you don't plan to use a keel, but still need to balance the decoy, one of the cleverest ideas I have ever seen is a teardrop shaped piece of lead about 4 inches long and 2 inches wide by 1/4 inch thick. This keel was developed by the great decoy makers of Stratford, Connecticut. One side is flat and the other is rounded off. There is a small hole drilled in each end. This lead weight can be screwed to the bottom of the center of the decoy and the small end moved to either side for balance. When correct, put a small screw in the other hole. It is best to countersink the screw heads in the lead to keep them from catching on lines.

There are any number of ways to balance a decoy. Try an idea of your own. I have seen old iron horse-shoes nailed to the bottom, yet this idea I would not recommend.

Hollow Decoys

A hollow decoy has many advantages over a solid one. For instance, the hollow one is less apt to season crack as there is air inside as well as outside. It is a lot lighter and easier to handle, sits higher on the water and can be made lower in profile. It will ride a wave instead of breaking through it. These are a few of the good features. On the other hand, it is more work to make a hollow rather than a solid decoy, yet to me, half of the fun and maybe three quarters of it, is in building the decoy, especially if you plan to keep it for yourself. Very few, if any, commercial makers bother to hollow out their birds. It would make the cost prohibitive.

Let's take a solid decoy all made and make it hollow. Remove the keel or balance weight so the bottom is exposed flat. With a pair of dividers mark around the outside leaving about 3/4 inch of wood on the sides and more near the tail. With a Fostner bit in a drill press, or even in an electric drill, remove the inside wood. The Fostner type bit is sometimes called a bread point. It has no worm and needs pressure from the operator to make it cut. It is made in sizes from 3/8 inches to 1½ inches. Any wood that is left can be removed with a hand gouge. Take the wood out as evenly as possible so that one side of the decoy will not be heavier than the other.

Saw out a bottom board to shape about ½ inch wider than the opening cut in the decoy. A board 3/4 inches or even ½ inches thick is plenty heavy for this. Lay this board on the bottom of the decoy and mark around it. Cut along this mark with a chisel or knife, or you could use an electric tool, making the recess deep enough to accomodate the bottom board. For making a water tight seam I use plastic auto body filler, and a few brass nails or screws to hold it in place. Sand it off after the epoxy has set up, then re-place the keel or balance weight.

If you had planned in the beginning to make the decoy hollow, the head could have been fastened from the inside, with a long brass screw before putting on the bottom board for keeps. You can hollow out the bird, put a 3/4 inch board float on the bottom (not inserted) and sand off.   This I do

FIGURE 41. Pintail head, life-size.

not recommend as it brings the seam very near the waterline and is a vulner-able spot for working decoys. Leaks could develop along this seam. With the board inserted, you have a double seam to help overcome this.

The heads on working decoys should have quite short necks. Try to make the birds look contented instead of wary.

All kinds of decoys have been made in the past. Some have flat bottoms, some round bottoms and some with the bottoms similar to the shape of the bottom of a sailboat. They all have their merits. As a rule, they have been made to work the best for the location and conditions where they are most used.

A knowledgeable decoy collector can tell where a bird was made, who made it, and the approximate time it was made. Shapes of bills, bodies, heads, and tails all tell their story, as each maker did his birds a little differently. A few tried to copy the real masters of the art and they had some

FIGURE 42. Black duck head, life-size.

success. Most gunning rigs today are made with plastic or cork bodies and the older wooden birds are being sought out and collected as treasures of art, which they really are.

Decorative Decoys

Many people shudder at the thought of shooting a wild bird for sport, yet they still enjoy looking at birds, and I find they prefer a man-made wooden bird to a stuffed one.

Decorative decoys can be of any size from tiny miniatures two or three inches long to life-size. I make my miniatures solid, and nearly always the head and body is all one piece. With larger size birds I like to make hollow bodies and attach the heads separately and at different angles. Decoys can be made with raised or partly raised wings, heads back, preening or any

PLATE 47. Swimming waterfowl. (left to right) Black duck, American eider, Canada goose, harlequin duck, and canvasback.

FIGURE 43. American goldeneye (top) and top and side view patterns of a northern eider (below). No scale.

FIGURE 44. Pintail (top) and harlequin duck patterns (below). No scale.

Drake   Old Squaw

NECK JOINT JOINED
WITH DOWEL SCREW

FIGURE 45. Old squaw drake (top) and mallard or black duck patterns (below). No scale.

other pose to show some sort of action. Probably more are made in the conventional "floating" style, but in less depth, because the waterline is the shelf where they are sitting.

Carve the bird in the same manner as the working decoys. Almost any kind of wood can be used since these birds will be displayed inside and will not be exposed to weather. I like basswood. It is free of pitch and cuts easily, and you can do wing tips that will not snap off. Any type of paint can be used on your decoy and you paint it similar to and by the same method as outlined for decorative birds and explained in the chapter on painting.

PLATE 48. Ornamental wood duck decoy.

PLATE 49. Folding yellowlegs decoy. This unique bird was made similar to many produced by the old masters for hunting purposes. The decoy is hollow and is shown in the open position on the following page.

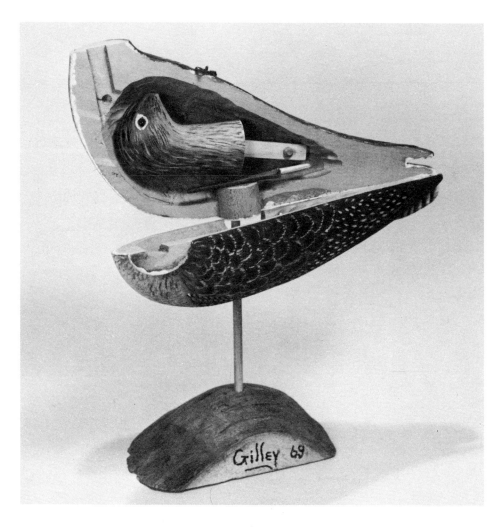

PLATE 50. Folding yellowlegs decoy showing hollow body and storage compartment for head when the decoy is not in use.

Pick A Project

Painting a Black Capped Chickadee in Oils

The chickadee is a bird familiar to most of us. It is the state bird of Maine, which makes it especially popular in this area. Chickadees will light in almost any position, so they can be mounted upside down or in any desired pose. I have probably made more chickadees than any other bird. Although I haven't kept an accurate count, I know they would number considerably more than a thousand.

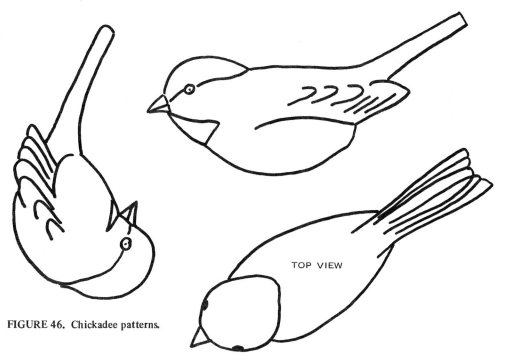

TOP VIEW

FIGURE 46. Chickadee patterns.

After the bird is sanded, coat it with Gesso, and sand lightly when dry. For a second primer coat, mix white enamel undercoater with a little ivory drop black (tube color) to make a light gray. Paint the entire bird with this. For a finish coat, give the back, sides and tail a coat of light gray paint made by mixing titanium white with ivory black (tube color). While it is still wet paint the tail, sides and wings with ivory black and raw umber mixed about half and half. A dark grayish-brown is the desired color. Now using a worn-out brush, make short irregular brush strokes on back and wing edges with dark gray with a very little raw sienna mixed in. This gives it a coarse feathery look. Paint the breast and side of the head with white oil color, letting the brush strokes overlap the sides. Paint the crown and throat patch with ivory black mixed with about one-third flat black enamel. The side patches should be painted a light buff. Use a long-hair irregular brush— the same type of brush that was used on the back. Raw sienna and white mixed will produce the buff color. Paint the bill with the same brownish-black used on the tail and wing tips. A few light strokes of black on the side of the head will help. Complete the bird by putting white on the outside edges of the tail, using the side of the brush in order not to smudge the tail proper.

How to Carve and Paint a Canada Goose

Complete the entire bird according to the pattern of your choice before painting. It should be sanded well and mounted on a suitable base. Adding feet, eyes, or mounting after painting sometimes mars the finish.

Give the sanded bird either one heavy coat of Gesso or two light coats. When the Gesso is dry, sand the bird again lightly. I use 100 grit sandpaper. If you wish to try burning in some of the feather detail, now is the time to do it.

To paint a Canada goose, the only colors needed are ivory drop black, white, raw umber and burnt umber. Be sure to have a good picture or mounted bird to use as a model while doing the final painting.

Prime the Gesso coated bird with enamel undercoater tinted with oil color. Have the color a little lighter than the finished color should be. Mix white undercoater and raw umber and prime the back and wings. For the black neck and tail, use flat black enamel. The breast and sides should be white with a very little umber added. Use the white undercoater as is near the base of the neck and on the rump and head-patches. Let this primer coat dry overnight.

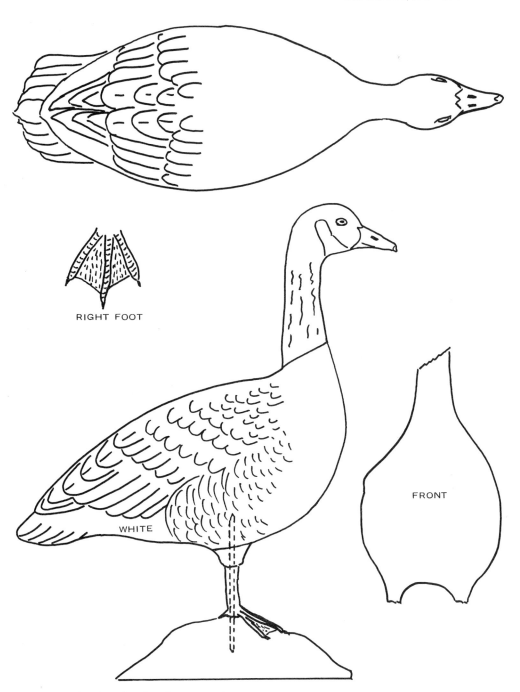

RIGHT FOOT

WHITE

FRONT

FIGURE 47. Standing Canada goose pattern.

If the primer is too thick, wet your brush slightly with paint thinner. Do not use oil or turpentine or you will make the bird shiny. I have been using sign painters blocking out white lately instead of enamel undercoater. I get a flatter surface to paint on for the finish coat. The flatter the base coat, the less shine on the finished bird. The feet and legs can be painted with flat black enamel to which a bit of raw umber has been added.

Proceed as follows with the finish coat. Mix raw umber and white for the back of the goose. This mixture should be about half and half. The tips of the wing feathers are blackish-brown. Draw the outline of each back feather in raw umber—straight. Apply a very little burnt umber to the shoulders, but don't over-do it. When the raw umber has set a little, say ten or fifteen minutes, use a soft brush, handled lightly, and brush from tail to neck. This will blend the feathers, leaving the centers a little lighter than the edges. Now give the breast and sides a coat of white with a little

PLATE 51. Canada goose.

raw umber mixed in. This should be about the same color as that used to prime these areas. Work this into a little white oil color painted near the base of the neck. Paint on the side feathers with raw umber which has been lightened just a little with white oil color. Make a few marks on the breast until you have gone over all of the lighter parts. Before this side paint sets, brush back and forth on the sides and breast with a dry brush. You will notice the resemblance to feathers. Now outline the back feathers with white oil color. Let this white set a little and then go over it with another dry brush. Make these brush strokes in the opposite direction—from head to tail. Brush very lightly.

Next paint the tail feathers black and the neck and head black also. For black that will dry fairly quick, mix about one-half ivory black oil color and half flat black enamel. Paint the white cheek patches and the white rump near the tail. Paint the bill brownish-black, the same color as the feet. Paint between the toes black and the bill tip black also. A few white intersecting lines on the sides of the neck will show up rough feathers similar to those that are on the live bird. A touch of varnish on the toenails after the paint is dry will complete the bird.

Small Minature Waterfowl

For anyone who wants to make small swimming ducks and geese, *The Birds Of Canada* by W. Earl Godfrey has some fine pictures which may be used as a most valuable guide. Also, this book contains several patterns which may be adapted to your particular needs.

These birds can be painted, left natural, or stained and waxed. If they are to be finished natural, I would suggest the use of wood with a bold grain such as cedar or pine. A very good simple wax finish can be had by using Esquire natural shoe polish in a spray can. Just spray the wax on evenly, let it dry and polish with a soft cloth.

While working on small birds of this type, I have found that a good way of holding it in a vise for carving is to screw a small block of wood to the bottom of the bird with two wood screws. Clamp this block in the jaws of a vise. Carving and painting instructions are the same as those given for larger birds except the work is of a much more delicate nature and requires great patience to achieve the desired effect.

Glue a piece of felt to the bottom of the bird when finished. It will be less liable to scratch fine furniture.

PLATE 52. Semipalmated plover (left) and Wilson plover.

PLOVER

SPOTTED SANDPIPER

GREATER YELLOWLEGS

FIGURE 48. Shorebird patterns.

Driftwood Lamp

A driftwood lamp can be a very popular and useful piece of furniture. To enhance its beauty add a hand carved bird or a pair of birds. You will find that a lamp of this type is very expensive if purchased at a gift shop or furniture store.

Make one yourself and show it to your friends. You'll enjoy being able to say "I did it."

These lamps can be made in any size and design desired. I will describe how to go about making a medium sized lamp with one bird.

Find a piece of driftwood, about a foot long; a piece that can be fastened to a wood base with screws. Saw out a base from a board of any kind of wood large enough to balance the driftwood. I prefer to cut the base in the shape of an uneven oval, but whatever the shape, it should match the width and length of the driftwood. Round off the edges of the base and either carve or smooth the surface as you desire. Fasten the driftwood to base, then paint or stain the board.

For the tube, use a piece of 3/8 inch outside diameter, copper tubing. You can buy a long shank 3/8 inch drill. With it, drill a hole from the top of the driftwood right down through and out the bottom of the base. Saw two slots about one inch long in the bottom end of the tube and bend both sides to right angles. Cut away excess tubing as shown in the drawing. Drill a hole in each flanged piece. Countersink the flanged pieces into the wood base and fasten them with small wood screws. Drill a hole for the cord horizontally through the base from the back side to where the tubing is. File away any part of the tubing that interferes with the cord. If the copper tubing is out of plumb, bend it to a vertical position. Check the size of the shade to be used before cutting the copper tubing to the desired length. A 1/8 inch iron pipe size thread can be scratched on the tubing with a small 1/8 inch die or you can use a 3/8 inch copper to 1/8 inch iron pipe size compression adapter to connect the electric light fixture to the tubing.

If you plan to make more than one lamp it would be economical to buy the 1/8 inch iron pipe size die and use it over and over as many times as you wish.

Install a rubber covered cord down the tubing and out through the side of the base and connect the ends to the light socket and wall plug. Wind some brown or dark gray cord around the tubing to camouflage it. Now carve and mount a bird on the lamp. Enjoy it.

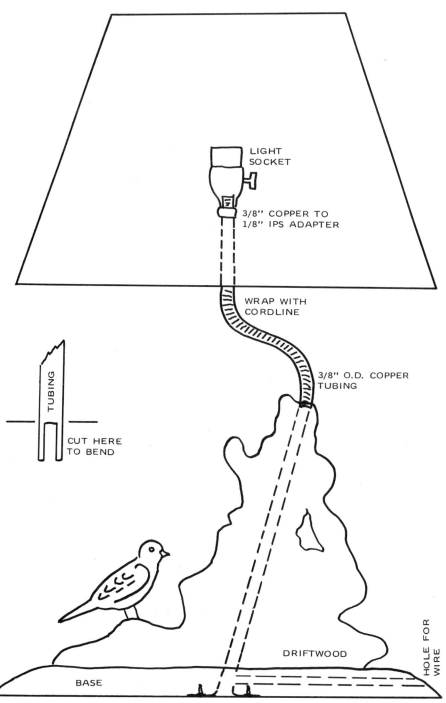

LIGHT
SOCKET

3/8" COPPER TO
1/8" IPS ADAPTER

WRAP WITH
CORDLINE

3/8" O.D. COPPER
TUBING

TUBING

CUT HERE
TO BEND

HOLE FOR
WIRE

DRIFTWOOD

BASE

FIGURE 49. Lamp drawing using driftwood and a bird carving.

Eagles

During the past ten years, I have carved about fifty eagles. Some were life-size, others were smaller. In nearly all instances, they were carved with spread wings.

PLATE 53. Life-size eagle with fish.

PLATE 54. A family of eagles.

FRONT VIEW
OF WING

FIGURE 50. Eagle patterns. No scale.

One particularly interesting model was a flying eagle with a goldeneye in its claws. This model was suspended from the ceiling on a wire. Air currents set the model in motion.

When the customer came to get the mobile, she said, "I can't stand to see that duck in the claws." I replaced the duck with a codfish and she was happy.

To carve an eagle, you follow the same procedure as carving any other bird. I work from a good photograph or painting, and I find an occasional visit to a zoo useful.

Except for miniature models, I raise each large feather while carving it, then burn in quills and smaller feathers. Eagle feathers are rough and stand out from the body. On the first six primary feathers, I put a slight backward-bend in the tips.

An eagle has pants and shows little of the leg. The first and rear toes are the largest, and the claws are nearly as long as the toes themselves.

The eye is set under a heavy lid, which contributes to the bird's fierce look.

Taxidermy

There is another hobby that ties in well with bird carving. A little experience at amateur taxidermy helps a lot. You learn the shapes of birds, the size of eyes, the shapes of wings and feet; close study of the different poses and attitudes of birds will enable you to carve more true to life. Also, you acquire stuffed birds to use as models for size, color, and feather pattern. Even though your first birds are not too well done, the shapes of the feathers and overall appearance of the bird is a great benefit. So many birds are found by the roadside that could be mounted and preserved for future use, it is not necessary to go out and shoot them in order to get specimens to work on. After a few of your friends find out you are trying your hand at taxidermy, they will pick up probably more specimens than you will be able to use. I well remember when I was doing quite a lot of taxidermy before I started carving. Almost any time I was away for the day, I would find, upon returning, from one to a dozen birds lying on my doorstep. There are many good books on the subject of taxidermy and the tools required are just common ones that nearly anyone has lying around the house. There have been correspondence courses in taxidermy on the market for years. Time and patience are all that are required.

Where to Market Carvings

I have been asked many times by people who carve, how do I go about selling my work?

The first consideration—is the work saleable? One good way to find out is to show it to friends and watch their reactions. Some will say your work is good and not mean it, but others will constructively say "yes" or "no." A few even may want to buy direct from you at a very moderate price. This is an excellent sign and it is wise to sell some pieces even though you feel you are not getting enough money to cover the work you put into them. This method will get your work in other people's hands—more people will see it and ask, "Who made it?" The demand will grow and then you can increase the price to what your work is worth.

There is one rule to which everyone should adhere. Always try to make the present carving better than the last one. This is very important. It is easy to let the quality slide, especially if you have a lively market, but if the quality is improved, the market (and price) will improve.

The best sales outlet is a small shop of one's own, but this is impossible for many of us; and where carving is done as a hobby it would probably be impractical.

Gift shops are good outlets, along with stores selling craftwork. Take or send a sample of your work to one in your locale or one that you know about in some other city. First, be sure the store is reliable. The owners of such stores will give you an idea what the demand will be and also how much you can expect to receive for your work. The markup tends to be high and don't be surprised if the store owner gets as much for selling your work as you did for making it.

One solid outlet is better than a dozen shaky ones. Never try to sell to several shops in a single area. The shop owner will be enthusiastic about your work if he knows he is the only source of supply for the item. Also, an ad in a craft magazine might be an excellent means of distribution, and in that way you would be your own retailer. And, of course, answer all inquiries promptly—this builds business every time.

Try Another

Now that your bird is completed, take an objective look at it. Yes, congratulations are in order. You have made a good start and although this first attempt is not perfect, you will be surprised and pleased at just how well it does look. I have been making birds for over 35 years and very seldom do I get one that completely satisfies me. There is always something I think I could do better on the next one. You are following a good rule if you strive to always make the present bird better than the last one. Before you realize it, you will find that you will be producing birds that will be admired by all who see them.

If this book has been a help to you, I am deeply gratified.

Now pick up your tools and try another.

PLATE 55. Ruffed grouse recently completed by the author.

PLATE 56. Life-size bobwhite quail.

PLATE 57. Scaled quail. Examples of the finished product.

H E L P F U L   H I N T S

Texturing

Try burning in the primary and secondary wing feathers and the tail instead of burning the entire bird. Grind the texture on the rest of the bird with a rotary tool or flexible shaft tool using a small V shaped emery wheel, a nail with several notches filed in the head, or a small dentist's grinding wheel. This method saves a lot of time and makes for more natural texture, especially on the breast. By moving the grinding wheel back and forth almost any pattern can be made. Sand the wood smooth before grinding. Small blue flat-head nails similar to those used on wallboard make good grinding tools. Sharpen them by holding a fine file against each side while they are turning in the rotary tool.

I find it is best to burn the feather marks directly on the wood with light burning for small birds and heavier lines for large birds with coarse feathers such as eagles. Woodcraft Supply Corporation has an excellent burning pen and another equally good one is made by Post Electric Company, P.O. Box 335, Andover, New Jersey 07621.

Painting

Prime the bare wood with enamel undercoater tinted with oil colors. Enamel undercoater is white and needs to be tinted a bit lighter than the finish paint. When the primer is dry, apply regular oil colors thinned with paint thinner. Use as little thinner as possible.

A simple insert for the bottom of the brush cleaner jar can be made from a metal jar cover. Punch the cover full of holes and place it in the bottom of the jar. Be sure the holes are punched from the top down.

Feet

Pewter is much better than lead for casting feet. It is expensive, but a little goes a long way. It casts well and solders with regular 50-50 solder. Unless you are an expert, use a soldering iron instead of a torch. By using pewter the claws can be cast right on the foot and shaped with a file or rotary grinder after the metal has cooled. This saves soldering the claws separately. They can be smoothed with a buffing wheel. For painting the feet use a paint made for metal. I buy pewter from T.B. Hagstoz and Son, 709 Sansom Street, Philadelphia, Pennsylvania 19106.

PLATE 58. Miniature wild turkey.

Carving

If you have wood that is hard to cut, soak it in water for an hour or more and it will cut easier. It will be dry by the time you finish the project. Don't leave the wood in the water too long as it might cause the wood to check.

PLATE 13. America's symbol, a bald eagle, by the author.

PLATE 14. Life-size horned owl.

PLATE 15. Resting bobwhite pair.

PLATE 16. Wemdell Gilley fashioning wild turkey body.

PLATE 17. Osprey.

PLATE 18. Completed life-size wild turkey.

157

PLATES 19 and 20. Flying bobwhite quail.

PLATE 21. Green heron.

PLATE 22. Pair of upland plover.

159

PLATE 23. Recent owl carving by the author.